Immediately Verifiable:

Essays Regarding Censorship

A Study While At University

By

Jason Judd

Third Printing First Edition 2020

This book is the work of Jason Judd as was written in part while studying
censorship in the MALS program at Madonna University, Livonia,
Michigan. I offer great thanks to all of those who might appear in these
essays, and also thanks to all of those people encountered along the way
while this information made its rounds. This book has had the text and any
content intentionally left unedited by others at the author's request.

     J.L.Judd   Immediately Verifiable

The USA Patriot Act:
A Moral Panic

Jason Judd

July 25, 2012

Madonna University

      J.L.Judd   Immediately Verifiable

J.L.Judd   Immediately Verifiable

The USA Patriot Act: A Moral Panic

It will ultimately be seen that censorship is defined as the exercise of determining the behavior of any people by controlling the information that's available to them. The media, what we read, what we see, what we say…it all has some influence on the behavior of people as social beings. We, unfortunately, form our prejudices and assumptions because of information that we're fed from others. The spread of information determines the focus of a group, i.e. where that group is going, how it behaves, and therefore what it believes to be socially acceptable – *righteous, true,* and *virtuous.* Societies form around the information that's available to their people. They form around the control and the accepted interpretations of that information as it is passed among those people. So, assuming that the preceding definition and statements have some validity, there is little reason to wonder why the federal government felt the need to control, in various ways, the means of communication in America shortly after the events of 9/11 with the passage of the USA Patriot Act. There was a loss of control of the infrastructure and institutions within the borders of America, and the people, as well as the government, were all caught by surprise. Did the authorities need to subdue some ensuing panic? Was our government's plan, when drafting the Act, to take advantage of some tragic situation in order to exercise powers that had previously been denied them by the Bill of Rights?   Or, did they really need to facilitate some means of communication between law enforcement agencies and first responders in the case of further terrorist attacks? Either way, the government, and the

  J.L.Judd   Immediately Verifiable

American people, were gripped with fear and felt a need to unite, somehow, in order to feel secure within their selves, within this society that we've formed.

In evaluating the validity of the Patriot Act, recent incidents in Detroit can shed light on the claims by our government that the USA Patriot Act has become necessary in order to secure communications for the safety of the people, made to question their security. In recent weeks, a bomb threat was called into the Detroit-Windsor Tunnel. That threat caused the tunnel to be shut down for about four hours, and much of Wayne County, Michigan went into lockdown while Detroit and Windsor police collaborated on the efforts to search the tunnel. Helicopters from the FBI flew overhead, and the NSA searched through electronic records. Police cars swarmed around the border as dogs sniffed through the tunnel. Security at the remaining gateways between America and Canada came to standstill. And even though an old pickup truck was hauled out of the tunnel on a flatbed wrecker, their efforts turned up nothing. They all responded, and the agencies communicated with one another quite well, I'm sure. But there was no bomb found. There was nothing but media hype, and pictures of helicopters and police cruisers, and news of a lockdown at the border. Like most bomb threats, a panic was created, no bomb ever turned up, and it seems now that such hysteria is even facilitated, while appearing much like a well-rehearsed dance, by the USA Patriot Act. A few days later, another threat was called in regarding the Ambassador Bridge which stretches over the Detroit River, connecting Detroit and Windsor. Again, the ballet of authorities followed. Then again, just a day or two later, a final threat was called into 9-1-1 during a Detroit Tigers' game, as the caller claimed that there was a bomb in the crowded Comerica Park where a

    J.L.Judd   Immediately Verifiable

game was being played. On the third instance nothing was even done. The people inside the stadium were not notified, the stadium was not evacuated, the media was fairly hushed regarding the entire incident, and on the following day hardly anyone around the city of Detroit even knew of the incident. In hindsight, they've never even caught any of the people who called in any of the threats. You have to wonder, while living under the government surveillance of the USA Patriot Act, which was drafted as legislation in order to secure communications to protect us from fear, terrorism, and domestic panic, how does someone call a bomb threat into 9-1-1 and target a crowded a Comerica Park, without the authorities being able to find out who is responsible for making the call?

In the modern day, most researchers can agree on the definition, causes, effects, and implications of a moral panic, aside from terrorism. And though moral panics in America stretch back as far as the witch-hunts in Salem, Massachusetts, they have progressed through the persecution of Catholics in the nineteenth century, the McCarthy Era with the onset of television and the Cold War, and even the hunting down of innocent people professed to be child abducting Satan worshippers during the 1990's, to name just a few incidents. The First Amendment, it could be argued, grants the people of America the right to be dissident, and the establishment in America, which conforms to tradition and norms, as people always do, therefore panics with the spread of news that their institutions and establishment have been threatened. The events following 9/11 have all the elements of a moral panic, and legislation created by the USA Patriot Act during that time, is just a symptom of such a thing. The Act itself, with all good intentions, could have been drafted simply in order to

　　　　　J.L.Judd　　　Immediately Verifiable

control the media and the communications in order to prevent some irrational social behavior that would ultimately result in the disorganized and violent breakdown of the establishment and other institutions within this country. The revised Patriot Act that was passed in the subsequent years (2005), an Act that was referred to as Patriot Act 2 for quite some time, the USA Patriot Act that is still in effect, intended to focus the efforts of authorities on the social behavior in America that could eventually fall into the patterns of some type of panic, or riot behavior, and it focused that behavior into some organized and justifiable nationalist mood that could not be challenged either from within or from without the culture of America. The Act solely intended to take control of Media outlets, and monitor any and all electronic communications, looking for dissent and widespread fear.

A moral panic is the result of many factors, and is an integral reality of American culture. The panic is typically started by some isolated and anomalous event, an event that is considered to be of deviant behavior by the greater society that has conformed to some socially acceptable norm. That deviant behavior, however isolated it might be, must be dealt with by authorities. The experts and authorities of the society will, typically, then begin profiling the type of deviant person responsible for perpetrating such an unacceptable act, even, as was said, if the act is isolated and anomalous at the time. The media, in modern America, will then tend to pick up and sensationalize the story, along with the profile given by the experts and authorities. A particular subject is generalized, and abstracted, and labeled as deviant. The people, who have started to spread some fear, or social phobia of that deviant behavior, even though it was isolated, then tend to relate other events, which might be completely unrelated except through

                                J.L.Judd   Immediately Verifiable

ambiguous use of narrative in the media, through generalizations and stereotypes until more than just the single isolated event is perceived by society. A class of events is constructed. The problem becomes larger than it really needs to be, there is some public outcry against the deviant behavior, and some legislation is generally enacted in order to deal with such behavior in the future. The problem is that the legislation is often brought in under prejudiced ideals, justified by isolated instances that are grouped together into some category through prejudiced values, and targets are made of some group of people who are ultimately seen as the subject of stereotype. The problem is created not only by the media, spreading stereotypes and relating what would otherwise be unrelated yet popularized events of immorality and deviance, never otherwise heard of by the population at large except through the mass media, but also by the experts and authorities who have adopted the method of profiling deviant people and groups in order to try and explain and resolve the problems of – crime, drug addiction, and mental illness in our society – deviant behavior. All of which seems to be included under the legal definitions of terrorism as it's determined by fear under the USA Patriot Act. This particular method of profiling by the experts and authorities in our society does not seem to be working (Adartey-Wellington). Levels of crime, drug addiction, and mental illness, all of them, seem to be on the rise since the adoption of this method of establishing American institutions has begun.

It might be argued that in drafting the legislation of the USA Patriot Act, in taking control of all the means of communication throughout our society, by securing anything that can be read, and in doing so by monitoring the media, Internet activities, and cell phone usage of Americans, that

     J.L.Judd   Immediately Verifiable

authorities might have simply been trying to stop the spread of generalizations, and profiling, of certain groups in order to head off any moral panic following 9/11 – before it ever had some chance to begin (Victor). The authorities and experts had no other devices at their disposal than to profile the perpetrators of terrorism, however unethical that might be, and with some target in mind then their best defense against some widespread panic would have been to control the flow of information.

Suddenly lacking freedom, the experts and authorities were forced to give the American people a new concept of what it means to be American. They gave us new goals and new ideals. It seems we were no longer expected to be *the poor, the tired, huddled masses yearning to be free.* And we were no longer expected to "throw off such governments" in those cases if the people of America were to ever be excessively taxed, or if we were unjustly tried like in the days before our Revolution. And it seems that, under this new ideal, we are to censor ourselves of anything un-American – that we are not to exercise those rights of free religion, or of free speech, or of press, or of assembly, or of redress of grievances. Americans are expected suddenly, following 9/11, with the passage of the Patriot Act, to be satisfied with the fact that we Americans are to no longer to feel secure in our homes, in our papers, and in our effects – in any way whatsoever. In essence, we were to no longer be Americans.

There is research showing that when some subjective reality is constructed through complex arguments and is adopted by the greater number people in a population, the few who remain objective and who try to point to the obvious error in the subjectivity construed by the majority, will feel some level of social anxiety in trying to show what is obviously

         J.L.Judd   Immediately Verifiable

objective and true, even though that truth is not generally accepted as truth by the majority. The dissident, who does not conform to the constructed subjectivity within that society, will feel some threat of recourse, and often the dissident will fear some violent reprimand by that society for not conforming (Ross, Bierbrauer, & Hoffman). The majority will continue to justify their beliefs and constructs through subjective and complex arguments, and the dissident will, more often than not, conform to what the majority is purporting to be true. However, on the most rare occasion, when the minority is able to see the objective reality that stands in opposition to their complex social construct as true, and it finally overcomes its anxiety and is able to show truth to the others, some of those who had previously conformed will begin to break away from the larger group, and as the larger conforming group dissembles then the perceived threat of violence against the original dissidents will tend to turn to a reality of violence perpetrated by the majority against the objective few as the larger conforming group tends to experience some shift in opinion, and as the leadership of the society itself begins to change. It is often seen that the perception of control is often more true to fact than the reality of control itself, and it is only the perception of control that is needed to change reality (Parker). Controlling information, it is evident in a society, is one of the best ways to maintain the perception of control.

The change in the accepted reality of the majority, we see, is brought to fruition by the collective action of the people, and that collective action can either be what is called routine or otherwise non-routine collective action. Minority opinion, or dissent, is typically found to manifest as individual behavior in private, rather than in pubic, settings (Santee, & Maslach). Those beliefs that are not well-understood or accepted by the

     J.L.Judd   Immediately Verifiable

larger majority force those belief systems into homes and to behind closed-doors until such time that there is a public need for that particular opinion to become public. If a situation is found where the minority opinion is some objective reality that cannot be denied by the majority, the latter having accepted some constructed subjective argument as its truth, then the minority opinion will gain in popularity and take some foothold throughout the majority with some kind of collective action (Moore). When society creates some social need for it, the minority opinion will be heard. Collective action can be one of two different types – and those, again, are routine or non-routine collective actions. Routine collective actions will tend to have some semblance of an organization, they will be reversible, and they will be typified by non-violence. Non-routine collective actions, on the other hand, are usually random and chaotic, brought on suddenly, and are found when some opinion that has been repressed within a society can no longer be kept down by the powers wielded by that authority. Non-routine collective actions are typified by violence and are often the cause of some popular subjective construct being challenged by some group with a minority opinion, a group that had been forced to keep its beliefs and opinions private (Nemeth). However, in the light of some objective and undeniable reality suddenly surfacing, being brought to the attention of the majority group, often through the media, the social change begins and the collective action occurs (Opp). With the reality of the Trade Center Towers crashing down and the horrific events that ensued, it is reasonable to believe that the USA Patriot Act would have been necessary in order to avoid any non-routine collective action, to avoid any spread of violence, riots, or further terrorist acts during the time following the events on that horrific day. However, if that is

J.L.Judd   Immediately Verifiable

the actual reasoning and driving force behind the passing of that particular legislation, and the fact that it was drafted in response to the terrorist attacks and an attempt to subdue any moral panic seems to be about the only reasonable explanation, then the question still remains – are the reasons for the continued use of the USA Patriot Act still valid? Most would dare argue under such circumstances – No.

Non-routine collective action, some acts that might be typified by events such as those seen on 9/11, are most often caused by the repression of minority opinion by the majority, creating a social anxiety that manifests itself in different forms. Non-routine actions are usually met by further repression from society, often through violence brought on by legitimate powers, coinciding with the breakdown of the accepted majority opinion and establishment. Some would say that the difference between legitimate power and coercion is the right of authorities to maintain some society through violence (Useem). Routine collective action, conversely, will often bring some sort of accommodation by the majority. Changes in legislation are seen then, profiling is minimized, and expert opinion is changed. Movements of social norms, beliefs, and activities change the widespread acceptable subjective opinion of the majority peacefully, and as that majority opinion changes so does the perceived reality of control of that society. Information seems the ambiguous key to control during such a struggle as that.

In any culture such as America, dissent is an integral part of the society, and the First Amendment even makes a grave attempt at protecting belief systems, as well as the rights, of those who dissent within our culture (protecting the rights of religion, speech, press, assembly, and redress of grievances against our government). Unfortunately, those Americans who

                              J.L.Judd   Immediately Verifiable

value those rights protected by our Constitution most, those who quite often choose not to conform with the larger majority who live in fear, have become targets of authorities under legislation like the Patriot Act. Media and writers are specifically targeted although they relate closely to traditional values. The inherent problem with such a thing seems to be that those people who most closely identify their selves with the values of any society, during times of change and upheaval, are those who are the first to protest in the light of any change.

Fortunately, in this case, there is a little known clause in the USA Patriot Act which is true after the authorities have gone to great lengths to get their one-hundred eighty-day warrants, warrants covering all means of some person's ability to communicate, and after the claims of necessity are given to the courts, courts that can't refute those claims of law enforcement, claims of some ongoing investigation that is imperative to the interests of national security. It is seen that once such evidence in such an investigation is brought to the court, the cause must finally be shown which initiated that "on-going" investigation. At the time that any evidence at all is shown in such a light, it is thought there will be evidence to the fact that the initiating reasons for the investigation can be shown as actually valid. Evidence of the initial cause must eventually be produced. In the hindsight of that on-going investigation, it is further specified that the initiating cause for the entire circumstances cannot be an act that is specifically protected by the First Amendment. In other words, something claimed to be an on-going investigation in the interests of national security cannot be found to have been initiated by an act of religion, of free speech, of press, of assembly, or of a redress of grievances against our government (Murray).

                        J.L.Judd   Immediately Verifiable

The question of leadership values becomes important when evaluating the USA Patriot Act in the climate of modern media, law enforcement, religion, and global affairs. The qualities of individuality, liberty, happiness, and freedom that have always rang true as American values need to be weighed against the reality of our security as a nation. The prospect that there could be a country that is open to foreign opinions and ideals, existing of the people, and by the people – some free haven for the poor, the weak, and the persecuted, should be evaluated against the fears that have boiled over from behind the closed doors representing the minority, but populations and opinions, as legislation has rapidly changed along with the acceptable concept of what is morally and politically correct in America. In becoming a politically correct nation, have we closed our doors and our borders on those people who need refuge within our country, a country that was always meant to be some melting pot for those rejected by other governments as well as lands of the world? Has America become some culture in and of itself, no longer just some ever-changing land of freedom and liberty, where the government is to be just the strong arm of those people who have been persecuted and expelled from all other decent nations of the world? We, as a nation, have become powerful under the ideals that founded this country, and it might seem unfortunate that some so-called American culture could ever be established, so to no longer change, while isolating itself from all other people of the world – a culture that sees itself as better than all others – as supremely American. The whole concept of America under the USA Patriot Act – conformity –seems to be, in essence, un-American.

We need to take back our country. Americans need to stand together as individuals within our rights. We need to

          J.L.Judd   Immediately Verifiable

exercise free speech, and press, and assembly. We need to voice our grievances against our current government at every opportunity – we do not have to sit still and be beaten. Our media needs to act responsibly. Conformity needs to be dealt with as what it is – a safe haven for people who live in fear of being repressed by social order. America needs to remain a country of individuals, rebelling against social angst, with a population that is ingenious, and each person unique. The concept of symbols in an ideal capitalism cannot be allowed to replace religion in our quest to remain a moral society, as what we value is evermore determined by the media and capital, and no longer by our archetypical leaders. We need to remember that the culture of capitalism will increasingly lack religion and strive to oppose the symbols of capitalism driven by insatiable fear. We, as Americans, need to choose to live in such a way, each of us an example, so to embrace a morality that is separate from our legislation, and separate from our capitalist culture. We need to grasp the fundamental ideals that have always made us American. We need to make it clear to our leadership, a leadership gripped with fear, that we need to be free in our homes, and in our papers, and in our effects, in order that the behaviors of individual Americans can manifest their selves in their own minority opinions. We need to be virtuous, and we need to remember the pain that is felt by all people, especially that pain of those who have been forced from their homelands at some point in their ancestry, and we need to remember that the freedom of those people who have overcome adversity throughout generations, and over scores of years, is what will always make up the might of the American people. America will not be, we cannot be, a nation gripped by fear – or some nation of cowards.

                            J.L.Judd   Immediately Verifiable

References

Colomb, W., & Damphousse, K. (2004). EXAMINATION OF NEWSPAPER COVERAGE OF HATE CRIMES: A moral panic perspective[dagger]. *American Journal of Criminal Justice : AJCJ, 28*(2), 147-163. Retrieved from http://search.proquest.com/docview/203526704?accountid=27927

Daniels, A. (2005, Jan 31). The meaning of a riot. *National Review, 57*, 28-28,30. Retrieved from http://search.proquest.com/docview/229701809?accountid=27927

Einwohner, R. L. (2002). Flag burning: Moral panic and the criminalization of protest. *Contemporary Sociology, 31*(2), 191-192. Retrieved from http://search.proquest.com/docview/60104191?accountid=27927

Humphrey, M. (2007). Culturalising the abject: Islam, law and moral panic in the west. *Australian Journal of Social Issues, 42*(1), 9-25. Retrieved from http://search.proquest.com/docview/61694057?accountid=27927

Moore, W. H. (2000). The repression of dissent. *The Journal of Conflict Resolution, 44*(1), 107-127. Retrieved from http://search.proquest.com/docview/224564363?accountid=27927

Murray, K. (2004, The USA patriot act. *Poets & Writers, 32*, 67-71. Retrieved from http://search.proquest.com/docview/203580415?accountid=27927

Nemeth, C. J. (1995). Dissent as driving cognition, attitudes, and judgments. *Social Cognition, 13*(3), 273-273. Retrieved from

     J.L.Judd   Immediately Verifiable

http://search.proquest.com/docview/229659282?accountid=2
7927

Odartey-Wellington, F. (2009). Racial profiling and moral panic:
Operation thread and the al-qaeda sleeper cell that never was
*. *Global Media Journal, 2*(2), 25-25. Retrieved from
http://search.proquest.com/docview/888154087?accountid=2
7927

Opp, K. (1988). Grievances and participation in social movements.
American Sociological Review, 53(6), 853-864. Retrieved
from
http://search.proquest.com/docview/60046425?accountid=27
927

Parker, L. E. (1993). When to fix it and when to leave: Relationships
among perce. *Journal of Applied Psychology, 78*(6), 949-
949. Retrieved from
http://search.proquest.com/docview/213943757?accountid=2
7927

Ross, L., Bierbrauer, G., & Hoffman, S. (1976). The role of
attribution processes in conformity and dissent: Revisiting
the asch situation. *American Psychologist, 31*(2), 148-157.
doi:10.1037/0003-066X.31.2.148

Santee, R. T., & Maslach, C. (1982). To agree or not to agree:
Personal dissent amid social pressure to conform. *Journal of
Personality and Social Psychology, 42*(4), 690-700.
Retrieved from
http://search.proquest.com/docview/839159564?accountid=2
7927

Useem, B. (1998). Breakdown theories of collective action. *Annual
Review of Sociology, 24*, 215-238. Retrieved from
http://search.proquest.com/docview/60066427?accountid=27
927

Victor, J. S. (2006). Why the terrorism scare is a moral panic. *The
Humanist, 66*(4), 9-13. Retrieved from

                          J.L.Judd   Immediately Verifiable

http://search.proquest.com/docview/235297692?accountid=2
7927

 J.L.Judd   Immediately Verifiable

J.L.Judd   Immediately Verifiable

U.S. Department of Justice

Federal Bureau of Investigation

Washington, D.C. 20535

February 14, 2012

MR. JASON JUDD

Dear Mr. Judd:

    This is in reference to your Freedom of Information Act (FOIA) request concerning miscellaneous documents. The FOIA does not require federal agencies to answer inquiries, create records, conduct research, or draw conclusions concerning queried data. Rather the FOIA requires agencies to provide access to reasonably described, nonexempt records. The questions posed in the referenced letter are not FOIA requests because they do not comply with the FOIA and its regulations.

Sincerely yours,

David M. Hardy
Section Chief
Record/Information
 Dissemination Section
Records Management Division

J.L.Judd   Immediately Verifiable

A Perspective on Censorship, Regarding the Patriot Act

Background – 9/11

I remember the morning of 9/11 very well. As it turned out, it was one of those mornings that my parents always spoke of, and I never understood them until that day, "It was one of those times when everyone remembers where they were when they heard the news." I was twenty-seven years old, it was late morning, and I had just arrived at the hospital near my house with my then-girlfriend who was of the same age as me, along with her six year old son. He was having blood drawn. We'd made it through the hospital and had found our way into the pediatric outpatient clinic only to find a dozen or so people crowded around the television there. Everyone seemed excited, but no one seemed to panic. The television showed the New York City skyline and the first Trade Center Tower all in flames, smoke bellowing. A few nurses in the pediatric clinic were bustling around with a curious eye on everyone, and I inquired to a stranger as to what was going on. "You haven't seen," the person answered with amazement, "a plane flew straight into the World Trade Center." My girlfriend and I sat down as her son was taken into the examination room to have his blood drawn for some tests which had been ordered. Moments after we sat down, the second plane came into view on the television and struck the second tower. People feverishly ran about the hospital trying to make their exits as best they could, not panic-stricken, but the mood seemed relatively urgent. There was talk on the news of a terrorist

          J.L.Judd   Immediately Verifiable

attack almost immediately following the attack on the second tower. The boy who I'd been helping to raise with my girlfriend was hurried out to where his mother and I were at, Band-Aid on his elbow, and though we lived in an apartment a few miles from my parents' house, we all drove immediately to where my parents were. I thought it might be best if I stuck close to family at such a time. The media was starting to panic, and apparently no one knew what was going on.

I knew I had to go to work that night. I was parking cars at the time, but I thought it would be best to stay with my parents for at least a few hours, and so my parents and I, my girlfriend and her son, we all watched TV, trying to figure out what had just happened. In the meantime, while the news broke, and as my dad checked the Internet, for some reason I dug out a pin to wear on my collar at work that night. I parked cars at one of the most expensive restaurants in town, and all I could think was that it was probably going to be slow for a few days. I searched through some jewelry boxes looking for anything as a symbol of my solidarity and patriotism, and once I saw it, I knew it immediately. I took the brass, five-pointed star from the old box of jewels and I pinned it on the breast of my shirt. During the next month or two as everyone in the media, the President, and the Senators, all donned their tiny pins of American flags, I wore this five-pointed brass star as I parked cars at one of the most expensive restaurants in town, in the front of one of the most famous malls in America. I wore this star as we parked the few cars-full of people who dared venture to such a place as that mall. For the following weeks, and even months it was desolate, and from the start I knew there would be war. Everyone was terrified to be in public. And a tragedy to capitalism, no one was spending money.

                    J.L.Judd   Immediately Verifiable

It might have been opportune timing, as the age of electronic communications was just at its dawn, but the incidents on 9/11 seemed to be just what was needed in order to give the government the right to take control of the communications in this country. About six weeks following that tragic day in September, on October 25, 2001, Congress swept in, in one single day, the USA Patriot Act. Granted, the Internet was no printing press, and the subsequent attitude of our government was no Inquisition, but the War on Islam had begun, and soon we had troops in Afghanistan, one of only two Islamic nations in the world, and before long we moved into the country of Iraq. It seemed, suddenly, that we had Iran, the Islamic Republic, surrounded.

It's hard to say what the intentions of the United States government were at that time. An Islamic fundamentalist group, Al Qaeda, had claimed responsibility for the attacks of 9/11. However, people can say anything, and claiming responsibility is not a hard thing to do. Still, America acted, and there is an unwritten rule in warfare to leave a standing army in neither any theocracy nor any republic (Machiavelli), so it appeared, by surrounding the Republic of Iran, we had declared war on Islam as best as we were able to do at the time. We seemed to diffuse the tensions in the Middle East as Iran was striving for nuclear capabilities in the region, and had been the sworn enemy of its neighbor, Iraq, for decades. It seems, we defeated that natural enemy of Iran to ease tension in the region. Still, at the time, I remember giving an oral presentation on the Islamic Republic of Iran shortly after the war in Iraq had started and I was marked down for ending the speech by saying that I think we invaded the wrong country, in Iraq, when we started that Second Gulf War. I had spent a great deal of time speculating on Iran's ties with Islamic

          J.L.Judd   Immediately Verifiable

extremist groups, and outlining some of their violations of human rights, and speaking both about Iran's drive for atomic weapons and their use of weapons of mass destruction in wars with Saddam Hussein. Still, the United States claimed to be in Iraq looking for weapons of mass destruction, and not in Iran, purportedly on a tip from Iran itself, and the United States never found any of those weapons. The whole scenario seemed a little bit too far-fetched for me to believe. And as turned out, in the process of obliterating Iraq's massive armored division of tanks which it apparently used as its only leverage in the region at the time, we left huge amounts of depleted uranium, in the form of anti-tank rounds, all over the Iraqi desert, and the depleted uranium which our armies used, the United States media failed to ever point out, was listed on those banned weapons of mass destruction that we had been looking for over there in the Iraqi desert.

The culture of Islam, forever at war with the symbols of capitalism, since ancient times and since the fall of the Holy Roman Empire, because of the irrational and evil behavior of a few extremists, was suddenly in ruins once again. Islamic culture is undoubtedly opposed both to Christianity and to the symbols of capitalism, true; and the culture believes that Allah is, in the end, more powerful than anything money can buy, but the culture also preaches a golden rule to its wealthiest believers; the rich who believe in Islam are obligated to take care of the poor as a duty to their religion. Still, the turmoil that the cultures surrounding different religions bring had once again surfaced in the world, and the United States, as we preach that we should love our neighbor as ourselves in this capitalist society of ours – based in Christian theology, and as we embrace Christian morality and forgiveness, we had seized the opportunity to destroy the natural enemy of capitalism, we

                    J.L.Judd   Immediately Verifiable

had declared war on that freedom of religion which had driven our founding fathers to fight for liberty, and we had decidedly declared war on all the rights of Americans with the passage of the USA Patriot Act.

We had denounced all those rights which are based first and foremost on that freedom of religion we once held so dear, and in turning over those rights which were clearly given to Americans by the Constitution of the United States of America, our government had seen it right that Justice could wield enough power to censor any and all communications in America, not only communications regarding foreign allegiances, but also any and all communications between American citizens themselves – anything which could be read – and it was all done in the wake of the dawning era of computer technology in communications, information, and media, and it was rationalized by pointing to the tragic events of 9/11.

The Reasons Cited - Our Government and of the DOJ

The Department of Justice, today, claims many reasons for the use and the continued need for the USA Patriot Act in America (Department of Justice). The intentions of the Act can be seen even in its name, which is an acronym standing for *Uniting and Strengthening America by Providing Appropriate Tools Required to Intercept and Obstruct Terrorism*. The Act intended to define for America both what terror is, and what acts of terror are. Terrorism, it seems, is a relatively ambiguous term, yet, as President Bush declared, it is an ideal that we were suddenly at war with. It is the position of the Department of Justice that Congress had declared a war on terror and so powers were needed by the DOJ, and the executive branch, powers similar in form and function to those

  J.L.Judd   Immediately Verifiable

used in the past to fight organized crime and drug cartels in America. It seemed that, in less tha a century, America had moved from fighting the Mafia, to fighting a war on drugs, to fighting a war on terror. It seemed that we could no longer oppose the cultures of European immigrants, and that the racism inherent to the war on drugs was no longer enough to sustain a Justice Department which already had more rights than the everyday citizen, so a new war was needed to sustain that lack of balance of justice in America – and we had found just what that need was, a terrorist act – a War on Terror.

It is still maintained by our government, and it is indisputable, that the Patriot Act was meant to facilitate communications between first-responders in emergency situations – primarily those of a terrorist act. Information sharing and cooperation is necessary between government intelligence agencies in order to fight its war. And it is still maintained that the Department of Justice cannot adequately fight the war on terror with its hands tied. The Act itself states that the government needs to be able to keep up with changing times and technologies to fight terrorism and to deter new threats, and so a number of sections of the Act require a re-authorization and re-evaluation by Congress in specified intervals which are determined one after the next (Electronic Privacy Information Center). Those sections which need to be re-authorized, and re-interpreted, by Congress deal primarily with the use of those roving wiretaps and delayed notice searches, which target an individual's entire communications network rather one specific device, all while targeting tangible items, i.e. business and financial records, and computer data, even if the notice to secure, search for, and seize such items is only given after the search has taken place. Acts of terror, it is stated by the DOJ, include coercion, arson, attacks on energy

          J.L.Judd   Immediately Verifiable

and communication facilities as well as federal facilities, conspiracy, racketeering, bioterrorism, dissemination of sensitive information, and attacks against mass-transit.

The Rights of the People

With all due respect to what is maintained by the Department of Justice who is charged with fighting the war on terror, many civil rights activists have taken the position that powers granted to our government under the USA Patriot Act are left unchecked, are far too sweeping, and they infringe on the Constitutional rights which were granted by our Founding Fathers long ago. With the legacy of Total Information Awareness that was left by the Bush Administration still intact, the government appears to have taken the position that if it is even able to secure any information, by any means, then it has the right to secure that information. People who work in information technologies' security are more aware of the government's attempts to secure computer data than most other American citizens, and they are left terrified of investigators, untrusting both of the Internet and of the computers they use. Tangible items, as described within the more than two hundred seventy pages of the Patriot Act, include hard disk drives, books, business records, bank records, and even library records. Many argue that to surveil and secure such things, an act which causes self-censorship as Americans have seen in the information security business, i.e. an act which infringes on the inherent character of in liberty, are a clear violation of American's Fourth Amendment rights, which allow us to feel secure in our "persons, houses, papers, and effects" by stating that those things shall not be searched without probable cause and a warrant issued only if it describes the places to be

     J.L.Judd   Immediately Verifiable

searched and the persons or things to be seized. Many argue
that it is difficult to simply describe communicable information
adequately in a warrant without just presenting that
information itself. Then nothing would need to be seized.
Would it? It seems evident that information is necessarily
protected by the Fourth Amendment. Why would one search
for information that is already known?

Also, opponents of the Patriot Act will claim that the
definitions of terror are far too reaching. Members of the
media, at the onset of the Patriot Act, were specifically targeted
by the Act because of their ability to create some mass
hysteria, coercion, and because of their physical access to
media outlets. For some time it was reported, even in a
statement by President Bush, that "anyone who causes fear" is
a terrorist. Also under the Act, conspiracy is meant to include
anyone who disseminates information about the manufacture
of certain drugs, i.e. chemistry and biochemistry. Terrorism is
also purported to include racketeering which is, simply stated,
the carrying out of illegal activities by an enterprise which
owns or controls the means of those activities (Free Online
Dictionary). Publishers are undoubtedly targeted. Libraries
and bookstores are declared to be havens for terrorist groups
under the Patriot Act, where terror plots could be devised and
where attacks are planned (The Department of Justice). In the
first stages of the Patriot Act, the ALA stated that specific
books were said to be targeted for removal from the shelves of
libraries and bookstores. The American Library Association
took the stance, almost immediately after the Act was initiated
and even more so at the time of the Act's first re-authorization
in 2005, that the Act was intentionally targeting intellectuals
and intellectual freedom (The American Library Association).
However, shortly after the re-authorization of the Act in 2005

                              J.L.Judd   Immediately Verifiable

the ALA was awarded a grant by the federal government, to be used to promote intellectual freedom, and the webpages which the ALA dedicated to raise awareness America's newly found onslaught of censorship brought on by the government in the form of the Patriot Act were quickly quieted. No one speaks anymore of the government's attempt to remove books from shelves in libraries and at bookstores; and the Internet still contains very little information about any happenings such as those in the past. The Patriot Act has been re-interpreted and the only information currently available, states simply that the Act had been used to target the ALA thirty-five times by the year 2003 (The American Library Association), how or why it was used, however, has been classified. The government will stipulate only that with information being so readily available in the modern day records need to be kept of who it is accessing any and all of that information. I was always under the impression that censorship was to be a function of family and religion, and not one of government.

Social Consequences of Censorship

Information is a powerful thing in society, and written material is powerful in the sense that it contains the information that must be shared among people throughout history. Still, even though information is subjective, and subjective even in its most fundamental forms, the data and those symbols used to communicate information are objects around which a great many social movements are centered -- social behavior, it seems, is reliant on the fact that people will behave with some sense of organization around an object of some form. It is a belief of most social scientists that behavior can be changed within a group by changing, or even by

　　　　　　　　J.L.Judd　　　Immediately Verifiable

removing, the object around which some group is focused. Throughout history, during wartime, censorship of written works has often occurred simply in order to alter the behavior of the groups who believe any subjects of those works to be true, and who have opposing opinions to the ruling parties.

Religion can be central to movements of censorship as well, if, in a subjective sense, the material presented in some work is morally opposed to some widespread religious dogma or belief. Censorship could also be used to stifle entire religious movements, such as Islamic Fundamentalism for instance, if one was to, hypothetically, remove the Quran from library and bookstore shelves, as was thought to have happened for some time under the Patriot Act. The inherent problem, undeniably, is that written material contains the history which is necessary for all people to form accurate and insightful opinions and judgments as social movements evolve. And so, as intellectuals become increasingly aware of the problems associated with various forms of censorship, and likewise, they become targets of any militant ruling political or religious leadership; and as intellectuals are targeted, it seems, with all of its objectivity, so are the sciences.

Censorship is common during those times of war when a nation must stand united, with no vocal opposition, when the people must remain homogeneous in their opinion, and outside beliefs must be quieted in order to ensure the righteousness of the reigning political or religious belief. The widespread availability of information in any society, as well as an opposing opinion, naturally makes the leadership in any society nervous, and so they tend toward censorship, and in the end of such a trend, conflict will ultimately ensue. The phenomenon was seen during the Inquisition following medieval times, with the advent of the printing press, and

                    J.L.Judd   Immediately Verifiable

quickly those with unpopular opinions fled to America and
founded our nation which was based on Freedom, most
importantly freedom of religion. The practice was also
undoubtedly seen to accompany the feelings of racial
superiority of nations during World War II. And, finally, used
as a tool, censorship has been seen in America with the onset
of widespread Internet usage in this country to promote
capitalist ideals. The written works and information containing
the perspective of the unpopular or opposing groups have been
removed from society so that the group's behavior can be
changed. The trend will continue, targeting intellectuals and
scientists, to the behest of the ruling parties.

**A Perspective Following the Re-authorization of the Patriot
Act in 2005**

      There was a sentiment in the media following the first
re-authorization of the USA Patriot Act in 2005 that there
would be no justice found within the unchecked powers of the
newly found intelligence communities. The ALA was the
most outspoken of any organization against the Act, and their
website reported the potential for violations of the rights of
library users nationwide. They reported initially that they had
been targeted by the Act thirty-five times, that the government
had given itself unchecked powers to remove books from
library shelves, and to conduct intelligence gathering and
surveillance without warrants, or checks, by other government
bodies, within the confines of any of America's libraries.
However, the media was quickly quieted in all aspects for
reasons of national security.

      It was shortly after the re-authorization in 2005, as I
read back then that the sweeping powers of the intelligence
communities had not expired as was initially hoped for, that I

                                                   J.L.Judd   Immediately Verifiable

decided to bear some of the burden in defending the rights of Americans granted by the Constitution. I decided that history could not be re-written, and that prejudice could be the only driving force behind the censorship of our media, which the USA Patriot Act cited as not only necessary for books, but also e-mails, cell phone usage, business records, and also any assortment of documents on a computer – not limited to webpages. The government, whether it was for just cause or not, it did not seem to matter to me at the time, had decided to devoid the public opinion of any argument thought to threaten the powers of American capitalism as an institution. America had decided to rid itself of its skeptics – those people who found it prudent not to judge simply for lack of good cause to do so.

Eventually, prompted by the misinformation that was being reported in mainstream media and having completed a course in network and systems security from Microsoft, and having seen firsthand the advantage that was being taken by the Department of Justice, I decided to enroll in a Master's of Liberal Studies program, in which I focused my studies on censorship, and the USA Patriot Act was found to be quite relevant to much of my research. It was only in this final term of that program though that I decided to speak up against that advantage which the government had taken, and all for only a couple of independent study credits. I began writing to various government agencies regarding the violation of the Constitutional rights of Americans which had been the focus of my attention for so long. At the start of the term, it seemed no one else was really willing to care.

A Redress of Grievances

This project started, going against my better judgment, in anticipation of writing various government agencies and organizations in order to try and determine for myself what was going on behind the Patriot Act with regards to the American Library Association. It was at the point, after several years of festering, that I needed to find out what it was that the media hadn't been telling everyone. The project started out in the right direction as I read that the Congressional Armed Services Committees had decided that domestic terrorism was suddenly to fall under the jurisdiction of the Department of Defense, handled in military courts, and would be out of the hands of the Department of Justice. The first e-mails I sent out were simple inquiries to a number of offices in the ALA. I reported to them in my correspondence that I'd read years earlier that specific books had been targeted under the USA Patriot Act within libraries, that people in fact were not targets of the Act, that I'd spent some years trying to be the fly in the ointment of such injustice, and I asked specifically which books had been removed from any shelves in libraries, as that was what I'd originally understood the matter to be between the years 2003 and 2005. No one in the ALA responded to any of my correspondences until it was far too late. Following a plan, I then wrote to my congressman, if for no other reason than to make him aware of the project which I'd undertaken, and I asked for the opportunity to have him help me in conducting my research, if he felt the cause was just. His response was also delayed. So, having heard nothing yet from anyone, it seemed to me that no one could speak on the matter. According to plan, I contacted the Freedom of Information Office within the Department of Homeland Security which immediately proceeded to tell me

     J.L.Judd   Immediately Verifiable

that their department did not keep any records like those which I requested, and then the contact which I'd made there, within the DHS, directed me to a particular Freedom of Information Office within the FBI. Homeland Security stated that the FBI should have those records that I was after. I contacted the FBI, kicking up dust, perhaps trying to make an example of myself, and I waited. I received a convoluted response from my congressman at that point which told me nothing. He gave me a vague and widespread opinion floating around Washington that something needed to be done to stop the theft of intellectual property – they just didn't know what it was they had to do. He didn't mention the USA Patriot Act in any way. I wrote to my Senator, again with the same inquiry; I was simply trying to find out which books had been targeted at the ALA under the USA Patriot Act in order to read some of them and compare how the material fell under the guidelines of the Act. That was when I received a letter from the FBI. The FBI told me that my inquiry was not specific enough, that they could not provide me any information on the matter, and that the FBI does not discuss nonexempt issues under the Freedom of Information Act. Their reply was short, but their response was imminent.

Some people call it terror, while others call it paranoia, but either way I've learned that those terms are but simple political jargon used to leave some impression of fear on a listener who might be trying to understand what's being said, terms which are used to make a listener's ego malleable in order to impose some undeniable response from him or her.

My mail was disrupted. I had my car broken into. Within the first week after receiving the letter from the FBI, two nights in a row my car alarm went off repeatedly. And though I was quick enough to not venture outside as the alarm

     J.L.Judd   Immediately Verifiable

sounded the second time each night, the driver side door was left open the next morning on both occasions. Another night a man who I saw dressed in black get away down the street, had apparently thrown a cat on the roof of my house which caused some commotion and which subsequently jumped to the ground in front of me; it made a tremendous racket and I'm assuming that the man I saw was again trying to get me outside. Then again, on another night, all while I was at home, someone could be heard kicking at my basement window – five or six times. All of that happened, I mind you, for some reason, not while I was gone, but while I was at home. I did have the sense to set up a security camera to record any activity inside during the day at that time. I only recorded voices in the basement on a few days, and images showing the door being opened for a quick exit on others. However, no one ever passed in front of the camera at the top of the stairs while it was recording, and nothing was ever missing beside the odd old hard disk drive. On different occasions, activity my local area computer network was intentionally disrupted for several hours in the house during the afternoon while I was gone and so during those times the camera recorded only black. I later found, at the end of those episodes, that one of my basement windows had been left unlocked by someone.

Eventually, I received a response from my Senator, who seemed delighted that someone took notice of the government's problem, that the Senate was aware of the problem as well, and that there was something called The Justice Act on the floor of Congress which would limit the sweeping and unchecked powers granted to the Department of Justice under the USA Patriot Act. Soon thereafter I read in a New York Times article that the Senate Intelligence Committee had started official hearings into the practices under

    J.L.Judd   Immediately Verifiable

the Patriot Act of the DOJ which had until that point been undisclosed. It was stated however that, for reasons of national security, the committee could not even disclose their findings to other members of the Senate, let alone to the general public, because the abuses and usurpations were so horrific. The topic has since fallen out of the news once again. That was only a few weeks ago now, and since that time, a political blunder – some Secret Service agents were caught not paying for their prostitutes while awaiting the arrival of the President in Colombia, and as the news spread, Obama might have quickly lost the presidency. The Secret Service might be sick of executive control as well, or so it might seem. I've decided to remain silent, like the government, since those things happened which I outlined here.

The Future of America

We are no longer free Americans. We live in a State of National Security. We must unite in order to regain our freedoms lost to the hands of terror. For as long as we are denied our rights, America is losing the war on terror. Censorship is, and always has been, a function of family and of religion. Any government which partakes in such practices like those found under the USA Patriot Act, even with the rapid spread of information at hand, is tyrannical. We live for utility, however there is no justice passed in present times on the ruling powers at hand. The greater good for the greater number?– so long as it doesn't interfere with the lawyers, the politicians, and their henchmen! We will undeniably suffer under such a law as the Patriot Act, regardless, and so it is our duty as Americans to throw off such a government, and re-establish an America, with Liberty and Freedom for all Americans. We live in fear. And what is it we fear? We fear justice because it no longer exists. We've been put down in our beliefs in modern America, and yet we've done nothing to warrant it. The First Amendment is quashed! And still we stand for it! And we sing 'God Bless America' on TV with cold hands over our hearts and blind eyes gazing up to those Stripes – peace and blood – which we've come to adorn with Stars, and here we are…America…remaining silent as we sing, but we've done nothing wrong. We've been forced into silence, it seems, for doing nothing but speaking up for our rights, America, and for ourselves!

References

ACLU. *Data Mining: Total Information Awareness*. 26 Jan 2004. Web. 22 April 2012.

Democracy Now. *More Secrets on Growing State Surveillance: Exclusive with NSA Whistleblower, Targeted Hacker*. 23 April 2012. Web. 23 April 2012.

Doyle, C. *CRS Report to Congress: Libraries and the USA Patriot Act*. 26 Feb 2003. Web. Nov 2011.

The Department of Justice. *The USA Patriot Act: Preserving Life and Liberty*. Web. 21 April 2012.

Electronic Privacy Information Center. *USA Patriot Act Sunset*. 18 Nov 2005. Web. 22 April 2012.

The Free Dictionary. *Racketeering*. 2008. Web. 21 April 2012.

Machiavelli, N. (1977). *The Prince*. (R. Adams, Trans.). New York, NY: W.W. Norton, and Co. (original work published, ca. 1500).

Quigley, B. *Thirteen Ways Government Tracks Us*. 13 April 2012. Web. 21 April 2012.

****Note: Public Information Officers are employed nationwide by the largest law enforcement agencies in the country. It is their job to have sensitive publications, those which might affect any ongoing investigations, removed from circulation. It is inherent to the nature of the topic of censorship that I have found some of my ongoing research to have been thusly removed from the Internet.*

Government Censorship On-line, the USA Patriot Act, and the Effects on Human Rights

Jason Judd

Abstract

This paper explores the various forms of censorship which have emerged in modernity with a growing global Internet. It examines and compares the techniques used by both the Chinese and American governments in order to surveil their citizens as they try to effectively censor what information is readily available to their people on-line. The effects of censorship and surveillance on human rights is discussed while considering the fact that the American and Chinese governments both claim to grant to their people constitutional rights not only to free speech but also to a free press.

Government Censorship On-line, the USA Patriot Act, and the Effects on Human Rights

Thomas Jefferson is quoted as saying, "during a climate of fear, Americans would resort for repose and security to institutions which have a tendency to destroy their civil and political rights. To be more safe they would be willing to run the risk of being less free." The struggle that exists between those who control information and those who wish to see, to an extreme, any and all information unbridled is essential for the growth of people as social beings, and the issue has been at the center of violent times throughout history. Furthermore, the

　　　　　J.L.Judd　　　Immediately Verifiable

struggle over free information seems to have increased by magnitudes during our current age of technology.

The recent technological revolution which has marked our present place in history brings with it, not only advances in people's capacity to communicate with one another over long distances and on mass scales, but it also brings a corresponding increase in the need for some people, and political bodies, to censor those communications for various reasons. It's generally accepted that maintaining control over information in any society is essential for those who wish to remain in power. At the same time, those people who can't, themselves, be considered politicians by others often find themselves trying to promote a free-flow of both information and discourse, despite their governments, so that society can evolve and so that the progress of society, in its most abstract terms, in its understanding of physical science as well as its social science, can improve, thus helping us to mature as a human race.

This paper will attempt to show some of the various forms of censorship which are in place around the world which are currently being used, on the largest scales, by ruling political powers. It will examine the censorship of China's Internet, look briefly at the censorship of the Internet infrastructures in place among other isolated countries, such as the North Korean and Iran, and also look at the powers of Internet surveillance which have been afforded to the federal government within the United States, powers granted which span all forms of electronic communications as well as anything that can be read. It will compare and contrast the means of the various forms of censorship that are herein described, and it will compare the harmful ends which are brought on by stunting the

 J.L.Judd   Immediately Verifiable

free flow of information on the global Internet, as well as look at the effects on society in general and what some political entities are doing to stifle any harm done by censorship.

To start, it should be noted that countries tend to maintain, in one way or another, their own network infrastructure, loosely connected, and once these are all intertwined, we have what we call the Internet. Top level domains, such as .com, .net, .org, edu, as well as those assigned to countries like .cn, .us, .de, etc. are all maintained by separate domain name services, and any Internet traffic that is outbound from some local intranet anywhere in the world is directed to those top-level domains by one of the seven root servers found globally. A country, Iran for example, if it wishes, can maintain a single gateway between the network infrastructure it has built for its people to use as an Internet and that of the rest of the world simply by controlling the network traffic at a single gateway or firewall. Any servers on the Iranian side of the firewall would be free for any user to access, while traffic between that server and the rest of the world would be controlled by the firewall in place, monitored and configured by whoever it is controlling the Iranian Internet. Globally, however, standards have been developed so that each of these large networks built within countries, and traffic to and from between top-level domains, can operate as one large Internet. Corporations, many of them based in the U.S., have developed search engines which gather information that has been published on the Internet by using technologies such as key word listings, or web crawls, so that a user in one place can easily find any information that he or she is looking for on a server at another place. Google's source code will actively seek out any files that are available to the public, while others such as yahoo, and MSN's bing, use lists

	J.L.Judd	Immediately Verifiable

of keywords that are made as the publisher of web resources
attempts to make his or her information available to the public
at large. As long as the networks stay connected through
networking technologies, i.e. routers, switches, and hubs, and
as long as there are root and domain naming services which
will direct traffic to web servers around the different networks,
then one large global Internet will remain in place. It is
believed by many that by maintaining such a huge database of
information, that which we call the Internet, which can easily
be searched by anyone around the world, society can better
evolve, it will bring people closer together, and those people
will have greater purpose and understanding. Ideas that used to
take centuries to evolve should now take days, and fortunes
will be made and lost in the blink of an eye, and all people will
be equal. Information has suddenly greatly impacted both
economic conditions, as well human rights, and this must be
why such technology as the Internet is so wieldy, and elusive,
for political parties throughout the world. Naturally then, under
political pressure, technologies for filtering and for censorship
have grown by leaps and bounds, while countries which tout
freedom, and liberty encourage those corporations developing
such censorship technologies to act responsibly when looking
at the human rights, and violations thereof, throughout a
society. But as powerful as our governments are, are they able
to do so while not being accused of hypocrisy?

While some nations use a single gateway to try and control the
information flowing across its borders, like Iran, and North
Korea, China's Internet filtering and surveillance infrastructure
is far more advanced. Their backbone is built on Cisco routers,
and Cisco has been accused of training technicians in China to
configure their routers and switches so that IP addresses can be

　　　　J.L.Judd　　　Immediately Verifiable

monitored traffic bound for and coming from prohibited sites. Cisco denies any wrongdoing, saying only that they provide the same hardware for China that they do for the rest of the world. Packet sniffing is easily accomplished and governments, the Chinese included, around the world choose to target individuals by using such surveillance techniques as they regulate Internet Service Providers. It is forbidden in China, for example, to research the massacre at Tianamen's Square while using the Chinese Internet. However, it is the targeting of individuals while censoring, and the violations of human rights that go along with such a thing that has caught the attention of many Americans, as well as many people within the United Nations. Subsequently, laws such as the Global On-line Freedom Act have come into effect and all Western and American companies have been encouraged to act responsibly when working with governments like the Chinese in its efforts to censor or surveil the Internet there. And Cisco is not the only company which has been accused of helping governments like China achieve such harmful ends that bring human rights violations that accompany censorship. American companies, i.e. search engines such as Yahoo, MSN's bing, and google have all been singled out for filtering certain words from their search engines. They have marketed search engines specifically to be used by the Chinese people in China, which use the Chinese alphabet when conducting queries. According to the Tribune Business News of Washington, there has been "considerable debate about the complicity of Western companies in building and maintaining China's filtering system (Johnson, 2005)." Simple words, such as "human rights," "democracy," and "freedom," have all been targets of Chinese censorship, and at some point in time, of filtering by American based search engines, like google and bing, that

     J.L.Judd   Immediately Verifiable

were marketed to China. Some human rights activists who cherish free speech are furious about such an endeavor. However, because of financial gains that are to be had, it remains difficult, if not impossible, to convince much of corporate America, and the rest of the Western world, that they should refuse to participate in those activities that end in such things like imprisonment of people for political reasons as those people seek information, or as they exercise free speech. The companies cited maintain that their practices do not constitute a clear violation of a fundamental international right. Their rationale is that the problem, as it exists, is the fault of the state, not of their own. They assert that remaining to do business in such countries is, "the lesser of two evils (Surya, 2007)," and that any withdrawal will "not have a positive impact." They also maintain that if they do withdrawal then more harm will come to the people's rights than will good, as the people will lose any chance at free access to information, or speech. And finally, those companies simply declare that they are simply abiding by local standards and laws, and that inevitably, if it's not them then, someone else will do it.

According to Radio Free Europe Documents and Publications (Cleek, 2010), as recently as 2010, in a single year, there were reported as many as 120 bloggers and journalists imprisoned under censorship laws worldwide. As a result, groups have been formed and projects undertaken in order to try and circumvent the laws of those nations who partake in such violations of human rights and free speech. In France a company named Reporters Without Borders has been formed and they have opened an "anticensorship shelter (Cleek, 2010)" where reporters can use an encryption key that's kept on a usb drive, as well as their credentials (user id and

          J.L.Judd   Immediately Verifiable

password), to access servers which have been configured to use anonymous IP addresses, and employ the use of encrypted e-mail so that those targeted bloggers and reporters throughout the world can access the Internet without fear of reprisal. One Canadian company, Citizen Lab, has attempted to circumvent the firewall in China by creating VPN tunnels established between users in China with other users in Western countries, and by mimicking network traffic that would typify currency exchanges, they attempt to allow Chinese users to freely use an Internet that is available to the Western world. Unfortunately, one Harvard, Ph.D., who was working with Citizen Lab while in China, gathering information, was found shot dead (Hawaleshka, 2006).

It is evident that countries all over the world have similar practices. However, China is unique in that it will not admit that the censorship even exists. They still profess that their constitution grants free speech and free press to their people and that they comply with what's been written in their constitution. All told, North Korea, Tunisia, Iran, and many smaller countries of the Near East such as Kazakhstan, and the largest being China, all seem to heavily censor information on the Internet for political reasons. They justify their actions citing religious discontent, and potential acts of terrorism. The question must be posed then, could what's happening in China be similar to what's been taking place in America since 9/11 under the USA Patriot Act?

Immediately following the events of 9/11, the United States Congress passed the Patriot Act in a single day and it has ever since changed the face of law enforcement in this country. It was called the Patriot Act to rally support, and it was

     J.L.Judd   Immediately Verifiable

successful at that. The Act was renewed four years later, in 2005, some provisions were even amended to contain no expiration. The Act was drafted drawing on existing laws that regulated surveillance of both telephone calls and snail mail in this country, and it applied those laws to Internet usage, e-mail, and cell phone technology. The problem that many people have found with the Act is that the amount of data that must be gathered and analyzed in order to conduct such a search of Internet traffic and electronic communications is so great that untraditional methods must be employed. And as the U.S. government sifts through terabyte upon terabyte of unsecured data and headers, thousands of false positives can be generated, investigations started, and criminal profiling of typically rational behavior can occur simply because of where information is directed to and from on an unsecured Internet.

It is standard that all e-mail messages, as well as any transmission to and from a website, is encapsulated into packets that include both a header and a payload. The header, to put things in simple terms, is essentially the address listed as to who data is being sent to, and who has sent it all according to IP addresses that are maintained by the Internet Service Provider, hardware addresses, the subject, etc. The header is followed by the body of the message, or any the data transmitted from a site which is called the payload. Different services on Internet, such as e- mail, file transfer, or web hosting, all use different standards or protocols which can be used to classify the data. So, in e-mail, just like the postal inspector can be granted a warrant to check the addresses to and from any particular address for a period of thirty days when sending snail- mail, so can the government check e-mail. And as the postal inspector can only examine the contents of

		J.L.Judd	Immediately Verifiable

an envelope if its addressing can be seen as pertinent to an on-going and current investigation, so are the laws of the Patriot Act applied to transmissions across the Internet. Headers of e-mail can be sniffed and examined with a warrant for thirty days, and only if they're found to be pertinent to an investigation, then the contents of that transmission, the payload, can be uncovered. The question then remains, which headers can be looked at with a warrant? Certainly, mail bound for the CIA cannot have the same rights of privacy as does mail headed for Walt Disney World's Magic Kingdom. An expectation of privacy still exists within the bounds of the Patriot Act just as it always has in criminal investigations. The people of this country are protected by the fourth amendment, the amendment which prohibits illegal searches and seizures, and as various users achieve a stratum of various levels of security, different rights are assumed by any user's data. Therefore, transmissions to and from an open wi-fi source at a coffee shop, or airport, or library, which aren't encrypted have little or no expectation of privacy, while transmissions from a residence that secures its services from a private DSL or cable modem through an ISP, and encrypt its traffic would have a greater expectation of privacy on, as well as to and from, the local network. Virtual Private Network's would then, with proper encryption, be afforded more rights than any traffic that traditional uses most Internet resources. Still, under the Patriot Act, like any other communication, a warrant can be obtained to gather the packet headers to and from a private residence simply because the information is being disclosed to a third party as soon as it leaves its own broadcast network, the headers are disclosed to the ISP who directs the traffic, and so an expectation of privacy cannot exist.

   J.L.Judd   Immediately Verifiable

Currently, in order to sniff packets, a method known as pen-testing is employed by federal authorities in the United States. Pen-testing removes the headers of transmissions so that only those payloads will not be examined until some warrant has been obtained. One problem with the Patriot Act seems to be that if certain patterns exist within the headers of that information that's being gathered, the addressing that directs packets to and from different sites, then it's quite possible that some transmissions can be deemed as a possible threat to national security for anomalous reasons, and investigations can be started which implicate innocent users in some form of international terrorism, all because of the direction of Internet traffic, of which many users have no real control. Warrants for the remainders of the transmissions can be obtained then, under the USA Patriot Act, and an investigation can proceed without judicial oversight. Such warrants have been called Super Warrants and once obtained they allow the federal authorities to conduct electronic surveillance on any network or electronic device that the person who is subject of the warrant might be using. The second obvious problem arise then. If a person is the subject of a Super Warrant and he or she uses the network at his or her workplace then does the entire workplace network fall under the guidelines of that warrant for surveillance purposes. The answer, unfortunately, would have to be yes. A single user cannot effectively be isolated on any such network and all the transmissions on that workplace network can then be surveiled under that warrant. Hence, many problems of human rights begin to unfold with the USA Patriot Act.

Despite the inherent issues with privacy arising as a person uses various networks while under surveillance in America, the method which has become known as Total Information

     J.L.Judd   Immediately Verifiable

Awareness has been employed to gather all data in the U.S. while using pen-testing methods. TIA makes an attempt at gathering all possible information, and sifting through it to find what it is that a person is looking for. Such a method exists because the authorities don't have the luxury of relying on huge amounts of incriminating data being stored on any network or system for long periods of time. There is quite often very little to be recovered during the course of an investigation, while any person is the target of a Super Warrant, so packet sniffing is predominantly, though not exclusively, used. All possible pertinent information is gathered during an investigation once a Super Warrant has been issued as soon as it's possible to gather such information. It's frightening that such practices likely and easily occur on the wi-fi network of the coffee shop you visit every day to check your e-mail and news. It's possible that you could be unwittingly be targeted by someone else's Super Warrant, and as a testament, horrifically, according to some sources, "Only 1% of the data gathered [by the USA Patriot Act]...is actually used in criminal cases (Glover, & Meernik, 2003)." Such a statistic could possibly mean that 99% of people targeted for investigation under the Act have done nothing wrong, or that 99% of the data gathered has been unjustly collected and examined while clearly violating what's stipulated in the Fourth Amendment of the Constitution of the United States of America, that which grants Americans the right to feel secure in their effects.

The actual technology employed by federal investigators was developed intentionally with the USA Patriot Act in mind, so as not to violate the Act, and that technology has been named, first Carnivore, then DCS1000; both are packet sniffing

     J.L.Judd   Immediately Verifiable

devices that can be configured to sniff everything from source and destination IP addresses from within the headers, to extraordinary amounts of datagram packets, and payloads. These devices can be placed on as small or as large of any network segment which is requisite for investigators to serve whatever warrant they've obtained, whether that segment is maintained by an ISP or is maintained as a private network. And as the warrants are obtained, what falls under the guidelines of that warrant, i.e. what can be surveilled, seems to correspond to whatever it is that the government is able to obtain In the post 9/11 world, it is important for users to remember to secure their data, and to encrypt network traffic and files. Again, all this surveillance happens without much oversight of the judicial system other than the issuing of the original warrant once some pattern has been established within the huge amounts of data is presented to them. And so, it seems, the people of this country are faced with an ethical dilemma. What can we do?

Open-source security software, all Linux distributions, and all usually Linux Live CD's have been developed and circulated for the purposes of everything from penetration testing, to network scanning, to encrypting and unencrypting network traffic, to shutting down port scanners which might be in use to analyze both networks and systems for open ports. Some common distributions are called Knoppix STD (which stands for Standard), BackTracker, and Knoppix Operator. They are all supported quite well by freedom fighters around the world, they cost nothing, and they are available for download on the Internet. With the technology and the code at hand which these Linux distributions provide, it has become hard to stop their spread, and there is very little anyone can do to deter their use

                    J.L.Judd   Immediately Verifiable

at this time. With some experience and knowledge of Linux, many networks can easily be secured from anyone who might be trying to penetrate that network across an Internet gateway. For more advanced users, some simple perl scripting can be learned and employed, which can easily be sent as a payload to any device which might sniffing packets sent from any network that's been secured by the administrator of that network. Again, however, once data is sent out of a user's broadcast network, without a VPN, to the ISP, the data is up for grabs so perl scripting can be used to disable any device that might be grabbing and storing payloads outbound from a secured network. The consequences of such actions, of securing a network in such ways as disabling a packet sniffer with perl script in the payload, have yet to be determined and are not written about. Perhaps one day soon someone will know.

The question remains, as we incite our vicious corporate machine against the Chinese government for violating human rights, as their citizens regularly end up behind bars for violating censorship laws, for surfing websites that aren't supposed to be seen, or for using search terms in engines that have been disallowed, is the United States any better at protecting the rights of their citizens? Are the ends not the same? Are we not targeting, unlawfully, and for no good reason, unsuspecting Americans who will only be prosecuted in the end by our judicial system, a system which had no say in how the investigation transpired? Will we not, ultimately, end up imprisoning innocent Americans, in this great land of freedom and liberty, for Internet activity which has been deemed impermissible if we continue to allow our authorities to operate under the USA Patriot Act? And while we allow

     J.L.Judd   Immediately Verifiable

such unjust behavior of our government, do we not, at the same
time, claim that our citizens have been given rights of free
press and speech by our constitution, just like the Chinese do
as they imprison countless innocent citizens simply for
searching for freedom?

References

A batcave of censorship-breaking technology. (2010). United States,
Lanham: Federal Information & News Dispatch, Inc. Retrieved from
http://search.proquest.com/docview/858992909?accountid=27927

Barboza, D. (2011, Mar 22). China tightens censorship of electronic
communications. New York Times, pp. A.4-A.4. Retrieved from
http://search.proquest.com/docview/857966001?accountid=27927

Caruso, D. (1995, Dec 18). TECHNOLOGY: DIGITAL
COMMERCE; the prospect of internet censorship raises troubling
issues for business. New York Times, pp. D.3-D.3. Retrieved from
http://search.proquest.com/docview/430425115?accountid=27927

CHINA: Internet censorship can be evaded. (2007). United
Kingdom: Oxford Analytica Ltd. Retrieved from
http://search.proquest.com/docview/192449626?accountid=27927

Deva, S. (2007). Corporate complicity in internet censorship in
china: Who cares for the global compact or the global online
freedom act? The George Washington International Law Review,
39(2), 255-319. Retrieved from
http://search.proquest.com/docview/219700666?accountid=27927

Dobija, J. (2007). The first amendment needs NEW CLOTHES.
American Libraries, 38(8), 50- 53,4. Retrieved from
http://search.proquest.com/docview/197191464?accountid=27927

Echegaray, C. (2003, Oct 20). ACLU director sees new threats ;
USA patriot act opposed by group. Telegram & Gazette, pp. B.6-B6.
Retrieved from
http://search.proquest.com/docview/268888416?accountid=27927

Feds say computer surveillance hindered without patriot act. (2005,
Dec 21). TechWeb, , 1-1. Retrieved from
http://search.proquest.com/docview/201561610?accountid=27927

Foster, P. (2009, Jun 03). China institutes news blackout prior to
tiananmen anniversary; print media, social networking websites, TV

     J.L.Judd   Immediately Verifiable

coverage blocked. Edmonton Journal, pp. A.7. Retrieved from
http://search.proquest.com/docview/250532970?accountid=27927

Glover, B., & Meernik, M. (2003). 13th conference on computers,
freedom and privacy. Library Hi Tech News, 20(6), 5-5. Retrieved
from
http://search.proquest.com/docview/201449487?accountid=27927

Haglund, R. (2005). What happens to the fourth amendment when
the usa patriot act enters wireless hot spots? Journal of Internet Law,
9(1), 12-22. Retrieved from
http://search.proquest.com/docview/229309561?accountid=27927

Hawaleshka, D. (2006). Citizen Hacktivist. Maclean's, 119(45), 129-
30. Retrieved from OmniFile Full

Janes, J. (2009). Censorship gets smart. American Libraries, 40(11),
32-32. Retrieved from
http://search.proquest.com/docview/197146564?accountid=27927

Kerr, O. (2003). Internet surveillance law after the USA patriot act:
The big brother that isn't. Northwestern University Law Review,
97(2), 607-673. Retrieved from
http://search.proquest.com/docview/233377055?accountid=27927

Korshak, S. (2011, Aug 19). Kazakhstan shuts down dozens of
networking websites. McClatchy - Tribune Business News, pp. n/a.
Retrieved from
http://search.proquest.com/docview/884302217?accountid=27927

Legislating cyberspace; in 2005, the eweek editorial board attempted
to carve out positions on important issues related to the growing
cyber-civilization, touching on censorship, privacy, copyright, digital
rights management and other matters. (2006). EWeek, 23(2), 32-32.
Retrieved from
http://search.proquest.com/docview/198558485?accountid=27927

Science and technology: Hidden truths; anti-censorship. (2010, Oct
16). The Economist, 397(8704), 100-100. Retrieved from
http://search.proquest.com/docview/758846121?accountid=27927

     J.L.Judd   Immediately Verifiable

Spevak, J. (1998). Ramifications of internet censorship by
institutions: What is legal, what is expected, what is permissible.
College Student Affairs Journal, 17(2), 73-79. Retrieved from
http://search.proquest.com/docview/224822889?accountid=27927

Stelter, B. (2009, Jun 23). Web pries lid of censorship a bit. New
York Times, pp. A.1-A.1. Retrieved from
http://search.proquest.com/docview/434106794?accountid=27927

Website tracks world online censorship reports. (2009). Newsletter
on Intellectual Freedom, 58(5), 152-152. Retrieved from
http://search.proquest.com/docview/217124374?accountid=27927

Censorship:
The Establishment of Morality
And the Conflict Within;
Modern America's Rewriting History

J.L.Judd   Immediately Verifiable

Abstract

Censorship was necessitated in social structures that needed to assign agreed upon value of good or evil to symbols found throughout society. This phenomenon was seen with the emergence of modern capitalism of the Roman Empire. The political censor at that time was necessary because their polytheistic society reflected little morality from religion and so it was reflected in politics. With the emergence of Christianity the Roman system of legislated morality began to disintegrate as such judgment of value was suddenly found throughout the religion. In modernity, it is seen that censorship caused by morality results in political conflict within a nation-state as well as within the psychological conflict of individuals. As censorship is often used by governments in modernity during times of war to spur the will of the people, as is seen in America's Patriot Act 2, unintended social consequences tend to surface. As an influence on the Framers of our Constitution, Jean-Jacques Rousseau is cited as saying that the will of the people should influence the law in a healthy state and not vice-versa. It is shown here that the Patriot Act 2, which has taken many censorship roles from state and local levels and moved them under federal legislation, will have similar psychological and social results as did those similar censorship laws in past movements of nationalism around the world. Such an effect of conflict is why our Constitution forbids censorship first and foremost while guaranteeing religious freedom in order to satisfy questions of morality.

                    J.L.Judd   Immediately Verifiable

J.L.Judd   Immediately Verifiable

Censorship: The Establishment of Morality
And the Conflict Within;
Modern America's Rewriting History

Censorship consists of "passing judgment of people regarding questions of morality" (Rousseau, 2009). The phenomenon is found in various fields of study including psychology, sociology, religion, information technology, art and literature, military science, law and criminal justice. In fact it is difficult to fathom any discipline not affected by or relating to censorship. The implications of censorship are found to be tremendous when researching the socialization of people in almost any way. In modern America controversial legislation concerning censorship revolves around terrorism -- that legislation is commonly known as Patriot Act 2. The second Patriot Act was first ratified shortly after the events of 9/11, known to Congress by the name *Victory*, and then it was renewed in 2005 with no expiration. The act defines for executive authorities those things that constitute terrorism as well as takes some constitutional rights from the people in order for federal law enforcement to better combat terrorism as it's defined. The ethical problem that most people have with the act is that acts of terrorism are defined loosely and it grants law enforcement unbalanced power under executive authority. Such definitions are written to include crimes such as racketeering, kidnapping, disseminating information about certain synthetic drugs, along with coercing and intimidating a civilian population. Definitions also rightfully include military and political references using terms like assassination and mass

          J.L.Judd   Immediately Verifiable

destruction, terms that might be appropriately used as they are during our time of war. At the same time that terrorism is defined, however, federal law enforcement is given the right to monitor all electronic means of communication without warrant, and use such information to curb any tendencies of the people against the nationalist sentiment of our war on terror. The federal government reserved the right to access financial and medical records of any person as well, again without warrant, in the interest of national security. And most controversial, our government has retained the right to remove any book from the bookshelves of libraries and bookstores, while reserving the right to conduct unrestricted surveillance in both type places. In the latest report to Congress from the American Library Association concerning Patriot Act 2, the ALA stated that the act has been empowered against libraries and library users thirty-five times, and the ALA urged changes in the act as they have determined that the rights of library users are being violated (Doyle, 2003).

The origins of censorship can be traced back to the early democracy of the Romans (Rousseau, 2009). Bureaucratic methods and written communication were age old already in the history of man, yet there had never been a government formed with representatives, a Republic, a ruling class, or a ruler who wasn't Godlike in nature. In ancient times, the Greeks had a government without representatives and every citizen had a say in every law. Every political decision was entirely sovereign and couldn't be disputed by any one, or a few dissenters, as rulings truly were the judgment of the people in general; morality of the people wasn't questioned by the government, but it was pondered by the philosophers. The Egyptians had a political structure that incorporated their idea of religion, and their Pharaoh was

          J.L.Judd   Immediately Verifiable

always considered to be last word on the morality of the people; it was ordained by their Gods. The Romans were the first truly modern political society in Western civilization. They were the first to be considered modern capitalists, and because of their size they were forced early on in their history to develop a Republic, or representative government, which consisted of an occasional dictator, but always of a Senate (Rousseau, 2009). There were structured classes, which it must be admitted gave powerful voting rights to the privileged few. Their system allowed for only those privileged to not only fight but to be enlisted in the armies because their early Pagan religions left a belief that the Roman Gods were keepers of the State and that to die for the State was to die for God. Those privileged enough to fight, whose votes carried more weight -- they lived in rural areas and were honored, while those with fewer political rights dwelled in the cities where they lived more modern, and what would be considered today to be, unfortunate lives. The masses of people living in Rome required strong politics. There were strong laws and enforcement of those laws. Managing a people in such a way required not only a Senate, but also a political body known as *the Censor* (Rousseau, 200). It was decreed that it was the Censor's duty to pass judgment on the people in questions of morality. According to Rousseau's philosophy (2009) the Roman religion, at the time of its inception though well suited for the morale of their conquering armies whose soldiers died for Rome and therefore for God, didn't leave Roman people with a modern sense of good and evil and so the censor was quickly seen as necessary in order for the society we know as *the Romans* to function. The judgment the Censor passed was not law and the only enforcement of that judgment was in the presence of the Censor. It can safely be said that the modern

                              J.L.Judd   Immediately Verifiable

concept of censorship can be traced back to the time of the Roman Empire and in doing so we see that at quite a fundamental level, at the very brink of modern society, the function of censorship was and always should be considered best to be *passing judgment on the people in questions of morality* (Rousseau, 2009). It was employed to assign value of good and evil to various symbols in capitalist Rome, and it was first incorporated because of their lack of morality in religion. To clarify, their morality was Pagan, as had been the Greeks, and morals were geared toward the notion of their Gods being in control of State while everything good in society was because of their Gods, and to die for the State was to die for their Gods, so the opportunity to bear arms for the state was reserved only for the privileged as such a death was means to the afterlife. Such a concept of religion left little room for value judgment in capitalism.

Taking Rousseau's philosophy into account, the notion of censorship was accounted for critically by the Framer's of our Constitution when forming a society. They took note of the idea of censorship when they drafted, most importantly, the Constitution's very first amendment, and it was because of religion, believed to determine the morality of the people, that censorship was seen as unnecessary, so out of necessity for all other freedoms from government intrusion the Framers of our Constitution gave religious freedom to the people first and foremost, and it was incorporated into the people's right to freedom from censorship. The idea of censorship as it relates to religion in our Constitution was borrowed from Jean-Jacques Rousseau's (2009) philosophy on *The Social Contract.*

The social values in consideration of governing a society incorporated into that amendment, that which guarantees the general will of the people should govern the

 J.L.Judd   Immediately Verifiable

state are those of free speech, religion, press, assembly, and that of petitioning the government with redress of grievance. The First Amendment reads as follows:

> Congress shall make no law respecting an establishment of religion, or prohibiting the free exercise thereof; or abridging the freedom of speech, or of the press; or the right of the people peaceably to assemble, and to petition the Government for a redress of grievances.

In Rousseau's work, he makes it clear that in order to remain sovereign within a republic, the general will of the people, which he defines in great detail, must influence the law in a society and that when the opposite is true and the law influences the general will of the people, the society must be in decline (Rousseau, 2009), the morality of the people quickly then being decided by politics and the sovereign voice of the people -- not heard. Our Constitution has been drafted in regards to such a theory so as to not allow such a decline to occur. So this "general will of the people" (Rousseau, 2009) in the United States had to be accounted for in the First Amendment with those outright additions to the Constitution of the right to free speech, press, assembly and that of redress -- or petition of the government. When taken in its totality the Constitution originally outlined the structure of government and granted a total of ten rights to the people; first and foremost though, it seems, it intended to forbid the government any right to censorship, or likewise forbid any hand in government from passing judgment on the people in questions of morality. It was written so as to prevent our society's decline as censorship seems to be an indicator of a modern society, as outlined by Rousseau (2009), which has begun its decline. In Rousseau's words, "Although the law does not

                    J.L.Judd   Immediately Verifiable

legislate morality, it is legislation that gives it birth. When legislation grows weak, morality degenerates; but in such cases the judgment of the censors will not do what the force of the law has failed to effect..." (Rousseau, 2009). It is explicit in the document that the Founding Father's signed that the Constitution is, in and of itself, the "Supreme law of the land," and it says that no law should be made at any level of government, or upheld by any court, to supersede the rights granted therein, which include that First Amendment, in order that our rights should prevent the decline that Rousseau predicted, and that the general will of the people should remain sovereign.

The Constitution is the rampart of American morality, the concept of such a thing – American morality, was purposefully never supposed to be a function of the executive branch of our government as it is under Patriot Act 2; there was never supposed to be a Sovereign of Good and Evil in American politics. The First Amendment was crucial in constructing our society in defiance of such a Sovereign and the amendment has been attacked in its entirety by Patriot Act2 solely in the interests of war. Modern capitalism is wrought with symbols that must have value assigned to them and traditionally, in modern capitalism, having well-developed monotheistic religions, it has been those institutions of religion that have always assigned those values of good or evil to capitalist symbols. Religious freedom is crucial, as are the other rights of the First Amendment forbidding censorship. According to *The Social Contract*, in order to live in a free state, as the Framers of our Constitution had in mind while drafting the Constitution, a society's ultimate end was liberty and, being necessary for liberty – justice (Rousseau, 2009). In Democracy, the goal for the people was to remain in a state in

　　　　　　　　J.L.Judd　　　Immediately Verifiable

which they were able to exercise free-will at any given time
(Kant, 2003), though they would give up freedom in order to
accommodate for the equality of others to the extent that it was
necessary for society as a whole to remain in its best conditions
– those of liberty (Kant, 2003) and justice. Such circumstances
make for a strong and free state that can be governed by any
and all people. The United States was the first experiment in
democracy as it co-exists with our modern monotheistic values
which include that of a standard good to which all other things
can be compared (Nietzsche, 2009). It can be inferred from
Rousseau (2009) that those rights we see as they are granted in
the Constitution give liberty to the people, and subsequent
freedom exists symbiotically with justice in our society, and
our liberty should remain unalienable. That is the premise of
our Constitution and, in America, it has been the rights of the
people, not the freedoms, which were taken under the recent
censorship of Patriot Act 2 so the events of 9/11 could readily
be dealt with. We will see that, nine years after 9/11 now, we
have an entire generation reaching adulthood that does not
clearly remember those events of that day and who cannot
understand what it's like to live in a society at liberty – free
from censorship. The generation which is coming of age right
now, has always lived under an entirely different political order
than we have who are at least a generation older.

When considering censorship in this modern light and
considering its psychological effects on persons, one might
reflect upon morality in Nietzsche's (2009) *Beyond Good and
Evil* so as, in retrospect, to see censorship in the neo-Kantian
terms that Freud did. One might realize that morality is
something tending to reflect the same in all people, take away
the pain. Some people can admit such a thing, all to varying
degrees, while others cannot, and so we are each our own

                J.L.Judd   Immediately Verifiable

person. Those bases of morality are where Freud (2005) seemed to get his censor, in his work entitled *The Interpretation of Dreams*, as it was there that the presence of his censor disfigured perception resulting in abnormal behavior.

In his *The Interpretation of Dreams*, Freud (2005) seemed to believe all people who are born rational are predisposed to an unconscious defense mechanism that might result in abnormal behavior later in life. Traumatic moral events experienced during childhood and which are stored in the unconscious -- repressed, along with feelings of lack of control and an inability to exercise both free-will (Kant, 2003) and self-preservation, can make a person more susceptible to the chemical reactions in the brain that lead to chronic neuroses or abnormal behavior (Freud, 2005). He also believed that those repressed memories, our unconscious *self-censorship*, result in not only a censored, but likewise a disfigured, reality that carries with it any corresponding emotions (Freud, 2005) of lack of control or misperception. Today, many in the field of psychiatry believe that only certain people are so predisposed and that such chemical reactions caused by stresses and triggers later in life are irreversible. However Freud, who is considered to be the *Father of Psychoanalysis*, seemed to say that with all people so predisposed to these defense mechanisms of self-censorship – resulting in these reactions in the brain causing abnormal behavior -- that it is possible that all abnormal behaviors, because they are the results of external influences, can be reversed by consciously analyzing their causal factors and moral traumas from childhood; factors which he found to be often present in the dreams of people exhibiting such behaviors (Freud, 2005). He thought that by exploring, external to the unconscious mind,

                    J.L.Judd   Immediately Verifiable

those repressed memories while under certain controlled conditions, the behavioral effects both of trauma early in life and stresses and triggers of later life can be reversed, as long as such analysis included overloading the chemical receptors of the brain associated with reward and not with pain (such reward included even a simple touch on the forehead during analysis). Such events, the moral influences which caused the censorship and abnormal behavior, were brought to the forefront of the consciousness and analysis of those events as limits under such circumstances could occur. It was solely for purposes of overcoming those censors, which disfigure our concepts of reality, that he found abnormal behavior can be reversed (Freud, 2005). It is the essence of psychology. Freud (2005) seemed to believe that because the chemical reactions that initiate such self-censorship in our brains, and so the neuroses that we call abnormal behavior, as they occur from external influences, while exploring those influences external to the censoring subconscious mind, and while circumstances are made correct for further changes in behavior, the reactions that initially caused the abnormal behavior, typified as neuroses, can be reversed. The cause and the cure would both seem to be the result of the external influence of morality and censorship. A major premise in Freud's work also is that it's not only traumatic influences, but those things we want and cannot or do not have which can result in such neuroses or abnormal behavior. All told in simpler terms, the phenomenon of censorship in psychology seems to be based on morality as well. In Rousseau's (2009) terms, a perfectly moral person would live "free from the sway of fierce passions, released from the tyranny of popular prejudices, but subject to the law of wisdom..."

　　　　　　　　J.L.Judd　　　Immediately Verifiable

There has been evidence gathered while researchers (Goleman, Kaufman, & Ray, 1992) have investigated the link between creative thinking and censorship that seems to support the theories of Freud and the effects of censorship during childhood on behavior later in life. Children, it has been found, emit theta type brainwaves when they are still able to explore the world unrestrained and while in the face of few prejudices. Only as those children are taught order and discipline and as they learn predetermined patterns of thinking are the emission of theta waves reduced and the detection of alpha waves more prevalent. Following such new phenomenon, as people age, it has been found that adults in a semi-conscious or unconscious state tend to regress to a creative state of mind and emit a great deal more theta waves than when those same people are conscious to their surroundings and aware of the socially constructed rules of society. It's been found that creative people tend to always emit more theta waves from their brain in general, and such a finding in children seems to acknowledge the fact that those prejudices, beliefs, values, and goals which are dictated by a society, and which leave people questioning their own morality, tend to change the function of the brain of humans in agreement with Freud (2005).

Freud has been discounted in many circles for various reasons, most of those reasons being political and prejudiced as his study of psychoanalysis is not exactly politically correct. He sees the problems of abnormal behavior we find in modern psychology to be a direct result of moral influences that lie outside the socially acceptable – the immoral, thus he seems to look outside the realm of the socially acceptable in coming to terms with those various behaviors. Society often finds itself a polar opposite to Freud and many people turn to the political

                    J.L.Judd   Immediately Verifiable

correct, and dictate the socially acceptable to resolve many of our conflicting social and psychological norms surrounding prejudice; it is being found however that those PC movements of self-censorship are not always as successful as they were once hoped to be. In researching psychological effects of censorship and self-censorship, as they concern political correctness, it has been found(Bongard, Burfield, Conway, Gornick, Moran, & Salcido, 2009) that those politically correct movements, although helpful in many instances over long periods, are often counter-productive. There is always a tendency in a politically correct movement for some people to exercise their free-will and not to follow suit with those politically correct group norms. It's much like those who typify opposition and defiance, behaviors we all tend to demonstrate occasionally; when we are expected to do something we deem unreasonable on its surface and only because of norms, we tend to feel a need to exercise our free will and defy those norms. Technically it's called *reactance* (Bongard et al., 2009). However, it's also being found that there is often an unexpected backlash at later times when attributing attitudes that surround politically correct communication to the fact that a member of the group being spoken of in those politically correct terms is present at the time of such communication. It seems a natural result of self-censorship. We see that when such a person being spoken of in politically correct terms is removed from the communication, political correctness follows him or her, and subsequent disparaging talk of the entire group being held in the politically correct light soon begins. Such disparaging talk, opposite of that when self-censored, stems from an unconscious disbelief of those PC attitudes and the self-censored PC talk which are attributed, unconsciously again,

                          J.L.Judd   Immediately Verifiable

only to the fact that a member of the talked about group was present at the time of the self-censored and politically correct discussion. Any gains sought through political correctness are quickly lost. Psychologists refer to such a phenomenon as *attribution* (Bongard et al. 2009). This counter-productive and unconscious disbelief of the positive attitudes we seek when self-censoring and being politically correct becomes easily seeded, positive attitudes become difficult to form, disparaging talk persists, negative stereotypes and the original social norms are reinforced, and the results are seen to be contrary to what the politically correct attitude had originally intended. However, it is thought that the movement of PC is not entirely lost in attribution and it is believed such attitudes can be generated from the ground up over time through example when a person from such a disparaged group finally overcomes the stereotypes of his or her greater society. On the other hand, studies seem to indicate, that such politically correct attitudes cannot be generated forthwith through self-censorship, top-down PC politics, or any such similar communications (Bongard et al., 2009).

On a cultural level, further evidence indicates that efforts of censorship with underlying undertones of nationalism during WWII Japan, similar in many ways to the Patriot Act 2 in modern America, seem to have seriously backfired. One shudders to think how closely it might reflect the attitudes surrounding American nationalism as we fight our War on Terror. In Pre-WWII years during the Japanese war with China and other Far East Asian countries there was a sentiment in Japanese propaganda that Japan was a far superior culture to any other. It went so far in Japanese superiority so as to even not acknowledge mental disorders in the people of Japan. So far, in fact, that a law was even passed forcing the

          J.L.Judd   Immediately Verifiable

sterilization of all people who had contracted what were thought to be genetic type mental diseases such as schizophrenia and manic depression while imposing severe penalties on healthy women who chose abortion during pregnancy (Matsumura, 2004). The existence of these disorders, however, were found to be increasing throughout Japanese society during the years following, contrary to what was intended. Not only were troops experiencing symptoms of traumatic stress, often known as "shell-shock", but such disorders were also found to be increasing in the civilian population, most markedly in the repatriated Japanese citizens from other Far East Asian countries (Matsumura, 2004). Whether the increased number of disorders at the time stemmed from social unrest due to the war effort or from stereotypes caused by censorship and propaganda prevalent in mass amounts and which targeted the countries those affected people had been repatriated from is unclear; all that is known is the increase in disorders was most prevalent in those citizens repatriated from the countries targeted in Japanese propaganda, and out of national pride for Japan, the fact was not acknowledged. In an effort to keep up the morale of the nation most of the illnesses that were coming to light during this time were being diagnosed by doctors as other, less serious, social afflictions constructed by Japanese psychiatry for the purposes of cultural propaganda, and the underlying belief that Japanese were not subject to the psychological effects of self-censorship, and so they were left untreated (Matsumura, 2004) during the nationalist movement. At the same time many dissenters, who were aware and vocal about the adverse effects of propaganda and censorship in Japan at the time, were hospitalized as mentally ill and not released until they made public declaration that what they had said was a result of some psychoneurosis. It

　J.L.Judd　　Immediately Verifiable

should be noted that similar public dissent of censorship during the same time period in WWII Germany, where conditions were more severe and less data remains intact of the situation, resulted in thousands of intellectuals facing the firing squad for the "offence of subverting the will of the people to fight." (Matsumura, 2004) The censorship and propaganda continued, at least throughout Japan at the time, and there must have been a snowball effect -- the suicide rate in Japan following the end of WWII in 1945, being attributed to such censorship during their nationalist movement, increased dramatically within a generation thereafter and today that rate is one of the highest in the world. Similarly, under Patriot Act 2, we might see an increase of neuroses – social anxiety disorders and depression as they onset in young adults while they mature in a disfigured reality, as they don't remember the terrifying events of 9/11 and they struggle with coming to grips with why our current political order in America is centered around fear under Patriot Act 2.

Censorship results in conflict, no matter the terms, whether it is a conflicted ego or *The War To End All Wars*. And war has no positive end no matter how much you'd like to believe, or like to have others believe, that a culture is superior to another and so it has the right of war. Social control through censorship causes abnormal behavior, which is effective in perpetuating a war through national pride, yet such control has serious long term repercussions. On the other hand, self-censorship through political correctness and encouraging peace, though it can have positive effects, also perpetuates disparaging talk and feelings of dissent by those forced to listen to PC terms in the presence of the group being talked about. With free will, we are undeniably a species in conflict. What do we do?

                                   J.L.Judd   Immediately Verifiable

> There are indeed times in the history of States when,
> just as some kinds of illness turn men's heads and make
> them forget the past, periods of violence and
> revolutions do to peoples what these crises do to
> individuals: horror of the past takes place of
> forgetfulness, and the State, set on fire by civil wars, is
> born again, so to speak, from its ashes, and takes anew,
> fresh from the jaws of death, the vigor of youth.

So said Rousseau (2009) who quickly goes on to warn such a state that, "Liberty can be gained, but can never be recovered." The quote seems to epitomize why many theorists agree with such legislation as Patriot Act 2 in the wake of violence. Conflict and censorship seems to turn over generations and some have just come to accept it as evil. In modernity, it seems, we've quite possibly become nearsighted in our technology and lost focus of those cycles among people which seem to persist yet require much movement in order to transpire. Rousseau (2009) seems to say that the sovereign state seems to exist only as the will of the people and that the "people [are] never corrupted, but [are] often deceived, and on such occasions only does it seem to will what is bad." Was much of what happened following 9/11 premised on deceit, including the Patriot Acts? It is a matter of debate. Social contract cannot be sustained when the legislation of a sovereign state targets its own citizens as enemies of that state. It is at such times as those as the law influences the general will of the people, and not vice-versa, that a society is seen to be in decline. And Rousseau (2009), in his wisdom, does not blame the people and admits, "Of itself the people wills always the good, but of itself it by no means always sees it. The

　　　　　J.L.Judd　　　Immediately Verifiable

general will is always in the right, but the judgment which guides it is not always enlightened" and as such those transformational leadership values of freedom and liberty will always prevail in times of conflict. Some people might disagree. However, it seems that free people tend towards justice and equality which will always remain a pre-requisite for liberty (Rousseau, 2009) and free will, and so as a whole, people, when given the opportunity, value freedom. Social order tends to stimulate acts of freedom, in defiance, as proof of liberty. Social order is maintained in a free democracy by people voluntarily giving up their freedom, not their rights or liberty, in the interest of justice so that all people can remain so free. It is just such a quest for justice among free people which destines those holding the transformational values of freedom and liberty to prevail, eventually, in any conflict, especially those conflicts caused by censorship that always have, and always will, take away the rights of the individual in judgment of value. We create our own prejudices and in such cases, during those times of conflict, it is seen, values of justice and exercises of freedom will always prevail in the end.

In speaking out of turn, the second Patriot Act could be considered by some an appropriate action to take for a government in a society whose social values are built around a framework such as ours -- it seems to be an appropriate response for a society like ours when in decline and faced with tragedy, and it's definitely an indicator of such decline -- the general will of the people most definitely having been subverted by law – but again, that the general will of the people is to be influenced by the law, as opposed to vice-versa, is most definitely contrary to the philosophy that the Framers had in mind when drafting our Constitution. And our apparent decline? It is not only the result of 9/11, where most of our

   J.L.Judd   Immediately Verifiable

legislators would assign the blame. Our dwindling population and our being known famously as an international presence both contributed the phenomenon quite readily -- that's aside from our internal prejudices generated through a legislated war on morality. And still most people would agree that order is maintained through such threats as that which the Patriot Act provides, so it's debatable whether or not order is the best solution during a decline such as ours, and we must be cautious as order can be a tricky thing. As Rousseau (2009) said when speaking of planning for national crises under a well formed government,

> This is the enjoyment of peace and plenty; for the moment at which a State sets its house in order is, like the moment a battalion is forming up, that when its body is least capable of offering resistance and easiest to destroy. A better resistance could be made at a time of absolute disorganisation than at a moment of fermentation, when each is occupied with his own position and not with danger.

Technology is an entirely different question when considering censorship. Technology often has a hand in the watching, and given its nature, in maintaining our order. Innovations in Internet security technologies because of Patriot Act 2 and because of policies in Far East countries where Internet censorship is most prevalent have created modern counter-culture. There exists a dichotomy between censorship by the government and freedom of people in Internet use. Although some innovations in technology help the political cause of censorship in countries of the Far East, such as China and Thailand, their counter-cultures foam at the mouth to grasp

                J.L.Judd   Immediately Verifiable

at pieces of censored information when they have such an opportunity, and those cultures spread such information through a well-developed network of users (Talbot, 2010). In America, similar technology, and the spread of free, open-source Linux security software distributions has allowed a technical counter-culture to ensure the viability of an Internet that can sustain a free flow of information (Lange, 2009) even under the watchful eye of legislation like Patriot Act 2. The morality of such an undertaking in opposition to censorship of Internet activity has spread, in America, even in the form of evolving and abstract forms of on-line communication; there are few generally accepted social rules and norms surrounding non-technical communication on-line, which could be because of its global reach, and so, such evolving communication tends to be increasingly ambiguous. Existing as it does, the young adult generation has taken to creating idiosyncrasies for much of the communication that takes place on-line today, thus Internet censorship, in such terms, has proven to be even more difficult an undertaking for the federal government than originally thought. We've seen phenomenon similar to this modern evolution of language on-line, which is a result of censorship, in American pop culture history before. The culture of hip-hop, whose music was targeted by censors for many years because of vulgar language and because of its tendency to stimulate puerile middle America with both militancy and ribald misogyny in order to bring about social change in defiance of accepted mores and norms, also created language patterns in the face of censorship that were not generally accepted abstractions of English when using proper grammar.

Censoring literature, as we've said too, besides influencing Internet activity, is one of the most common forms

          J.L.Judd   Immediately Verifiable

of censorship under Patriot Act 2, and quite notably of censorship in general. Throughout American history, literature has traditionally been censored or banned at the state and local levels, however, in modernity, as was said, it's been reported to Congress by the American Library Association (Doyle, 2003) that Patriot Act 2 has been used in such an arena as a library by the federal government thirty-five times. In interests of national security, one can only imagine how the act was used by our government in such cases, and one can only further assume that such books which have been targeted are scientific, political, religious, or historical in nature – the data is not intact. We have seen in the past that such censorship of fiction in literature should only backfire with graphic novels like *Lolita* as proof. Nabokov, in writing his 1955 novel *Lolita,* at a time when profane language was being censored in literature, took it upon himself while studying other works in sexual imagery and while teaching at Cornell University, used purely Freudian imputation to tell his tale. The result was illicit and the story of an aberrantly deranged man and a rakishly louche young girl was told while avoiding vulgar language and profanity (Glass, 2009). It was horrifically immoral and quickly profanity in literature was no longer so censored. Other books which suddenly then liberally used profanity led the way in literature for the new cultural movement. William S. Burroughs, a Harvard graduate, followed in 1959, the movement taking hold nearly a generation after the censorship of WWII that must have gripped even America while still leaving scarce data, by publishing *The Naked Lunch* forcing Congress to pass obscenity laws that prohibited obscene and profane material from being sent through the U.S. mail. Burroughs had quickly become the mentor for Jack Kerouac and Allen Ginsberg, and

                J.L.Judd   Immediately Verifiable

between the three a new counter-culture formed and began what has become known as the "beat" generation which changed American popular culture forever. And finally, when the movement hit the racks and shelves of popular fiction, Kurt Vonnegut gave the final word for popular authors in 1969 with his controversial use of one single profane term in his graphic novel written in protest of war, *Slaughterhouse Five*.

Still, we must consider the effects of any media on the health of our children, and although there is definitely some correlation between uncensored media images and health, studies have not yet been able to find that such a relation is one of cause and effect. In other words, although the two seem to coincide in proportion to one another considering the amount of exposure to such uncensored stimuli, they cannot find that such media actually causes any health problems (Sargent, 2009). It should be clear that media is not the enemy to fear in our War on Terror. Ordinarily they are seeing that the choice of being in contact with such uncensored media and any health problems studied in children are both direct results of other outside social influences. With consideration for morality the recommendation of most experts, with technologies like the television V-chip and parental Internet controls both standard in conjunction with current rating systems, is that the power of censorship in the home should remain in the hands of parents (Sargent, 2009).

With respect for politics, this abstract concerning censorship, morality, conflict, the First Amendment, and Patriot Act 2, should appropriately be ended now before going too far. And for reasons of liberty and justice it should be ended with those words said by millions of children, day after day, for more than a generation -- with those words long forgotten in schools today -- censored for religious reasons.

          J.L.Judd   Immediately Verifiable

And with these words it should all be clear: "I pledge
allegiance to the flag of the United States of America, and to
the Republic for which it stands one nation, under God,
indivisible, with liberty and justice for all."

          J.L.Judd   Immediately Verifiable

References

Bongard, K., Burfiend, C., Conway, L., Gornick, L., Moran, M., Salcido, A. (2009). When Self-Censorship Norms Backfire: The Manufacturing of Positive Communication and Its Ironic Consequences for the Perceptions of Groups. *Basic and Applied Social Psychology*, 31, 335-347. Retrieved November 21, 2010 from FirstSearch ECO Journals. (Document ID: 10.1080/01973509033317169).

Doyle, C. (2003, Feb. 26). CRS Report for Congress, Libraries and the USA Patriot Act. Retrieved from http://www.ala.org/ala/issuesadvocacy/advacocy/federallegislation/theusapatriotact/CRS215librariesanalysis.

Freud, S. (2005). *The Interpretation of Dreams*. (Brill, A., Trans.). New York, NY: Barnes & Noble Classics. (Original work published in 1899).

Glass, L. (2009). Sense and Censorship [review of Columbus: Ohio State University Press, 2008. *The Artistic Censoring of Sexuality: Fantasy and Judgment in the Twentieth Century Novel*]. Twentieth Century Literature, 55(2), 262-268,4. Retrieved November 21, 2010, from Humanities Module. (Document ID: 1985517521).

Goleman, D., Kaufman, P., & Ray, M. (March, 1992). The Art of Creativity. *Psychology Today*, 25(2), 40-47. Retrieved November 21, 2010, from ABI/INFORM Global. (Document ID: 1778787).

Matsumura, J. (2004). State Propaganda and Mental Disorders: The Issue of Psychiatric Casualties among Japanese Soldiers during the Asia-Pacific War. *Bulletin of the History of Medicine*, 78(4), 804-35. Retrieved November 21, 2010, from Sciences Module. (Document ID: 769075591).

Kant, I. *The Critique of Pure Reason* (Meiklejohn, J., Trans.). Available from the Project Gutenberg Etext (July, 2003). Downloaded from http://www.gutenberg.org/ebooks/4280.

Lange, P. (2009). Conversational Morality and Information Circulation: How Tacit Notions about Good and Evil Influence Online Knowledge Exchange. *Human Organization*, 68(2), 218-229. Retrieved November 21, 2010, from ABI/INFORM Global. (Document ID: 1768488301).

Nietzsche, F. (2009) Beyond Good and Evil. *The Essential Friedrich Nietzsche Collection*. Available from http://www.amazon.com/Essential-Friedrich-Nietzsche-Collection-

ebook/dp/B002GWUX6Q/ref=sr_1_1?ie=UTF8&m=AG56TWVU5
XWC2&s=digital-text&qid=1292134027&sr=1-1-spell.

Rousseau, J. (2009). The Social Contract (Cole, H., Douglas, G., Trans.).
Works Of Jean-Jacques Rousseau From Mobile Reference v.12.1.
SoundTells, LLC. Available from http://www.amazon.com/Jean-
Jacques-Rousseau-Confessions-Contract-
ebook/dp/B000Z4JQMO/ref=sr_1_1?ie=UTF8&m=AG56TWVU5X
WC2&s=digital-text&qid=1292134223&sr=1-1.

Sargent, J. (2009). Getting a Handle on the Media: Where Should We Focus
Our Efforts? *Academic Pediatrics*, 9(5), 289-90. Retrieved
November 21, 2010, from Children's Module. (Document
ID: 1957735071).

Talbot, D. (2010, May). China's Internet Paradox. *Technology
Review*, 113(3), 62-67. Retrieved November 21, 2010, from
ABI/INFORM Global. (Document ID: 2063109151).

Doc's Office

J.L.Judd   Immediately Verifiable

J.L.Judd   Immediately Verifiable

Doc's Office

Introduction

"Doc's Office" is an attempt to create a short story which might be controversial to the point of censorship. It draws from many pieces of literature which came before it, which have been banned, which deal with a deviant class of society, and which lack the use of profanity. If a reader cares to look at the bibliography, he or she will see references to works like Burgess' *A Clockwork Orange*, Dostoyevsky's *Notes from the Underground*, Nabakov's *Lolita*, as well as some others that might be more contemporary. However, most of the direction for the short story that follows was taken from readings in a class in psycholinguistics.

As the following short story relates to mental health, and because some people might take offense to its nature -- which is intended to open the eyes of the great majority to the injustices found within the mental health industry, I'd like to begin this short piece by mentioning that I am personally quite active in advocacy for those who suffer from mental illness, and that I volunteer my time, and participate in public speaking activities for, advocacy groups for the mentally ill state-wide. With that being said, I've heard many stories, and I've seen the many faces of mental illness, and I've been able to incorporate the many years of experience that I've had in the mental health industry, voluntary or otherwise, into this short piece, "Doc's Office". Fortunately, while writing this piece I was able to participate in some studies of psycho- and socio- linguistics, which is where a majority of the material which was fabricated for "Doc's Office" has come from.

            J.L.Judd   Immediately Verifiable

Much research has gone into the relationship between cognition and language. Repetitious, and non-specific, patterns of speech were used in the most common forms of language such as noun and verb. Run-on sentences were occasionally used to represent the height of what might be a manic episode, typical of Dostoyevsky's banned works. The arbitrariness of language, which is exemplified in *A Clockwork Orange* has been incorporated with the use of the DSM-IV schedules. Some words have been used in such ways as to be "medium frequency rhyming words." The use of medium frequency rhyming can be typical among some mentally ill who have language problems because those rhyming words are the most recognizable to them, and those words, it is said, are the easiest for them to recall. One example would be, "Ask a silly question, and what a git gives are answers like these." The words, "git gives," are medium frequency rhyming. It seems like a mistake to most people, but with further investigation into the word git, one might find that the sentence is grammatically correct. I've incorporated such language at points throughout "Doc's Office" in order to give the impression of schizophrenia, and in order to be upsetting to the reader, who might tend to think that such language is incorrect.

I hope that readers of "Doc's Office" might find it in their hearts to see the discrimination that can found throughout the mental health field more clearly, and for what it really is – discrimination. We've come a long way, though we haven't come as far as some people would like to believe, since the time when people with mental illness were indefinitely held in hospitals, the days just before Sigmund Freud began treating patients from all around the world with opiates and cocaine. Mental illness has been found to touch upon more and more lives during the last forty years, and we've come a long way

   J.L.Judd   Immediately Verifiable

from the days of the sixties and seventies when our minds were thought to have "opened". More recently, thanks to research in universities and at pharmaceutical companies, the medications used to treat mental illness in just the last fifteen years have advanced in bounding steps, and the medicines for psychology experiments which were brewed in the backs of bars during the seventies have been left -- to certain social circles -- far behind.

In America, and throughout the world, we seem to be living increasingly immoral lives, and our mental health seems to reflect such a trend of people being immersed in an immoral and uncaring society. The most recent number is that one person of five in the U.S. will suffer from serious mental illness at some point in his or her life, and as the number of people who are touched by such a disease is growing, as socially constructed as it is, we must do everything that we can in order to end the stigma associated with words like *schizophrenia, obsessive compulsive disorder, neurosis, psychosis, schizoaffective disorder, bipolar disorder,* or *clinical depression.*

Jason Judd
May 2, 2011

     J.L.Judd   Immediately Verifiable

Doc's Office

I notice for the first time that it's a sterile waiting room. I imagine it doesn't resemble those you see on TV. On the television you see them all the time. Those were waiting rooms. The room that I'm in right now, this is not a waiting room as far as I can tell. But I wait here. It's a cesspool for my brain here, though in my time just waiting -- I seem to have come a long way, or so people say. People make fun of doctors, and they make fun of patients like me. I learned that while I've waited. They make fun of me -- waiting. "What are you waiting for?" they ask me. I don't answer, but I look at them, at the others who wait. They think something's wrong with me, I know. "Me? Me?" Yes, me. No, I haven't known a lot of doctors. This Doc is the only one I've ever had. I've seen him for years. He's just Doc, if you ask me. I've always called him just Doc. I've only known his waiting rooms, and no one else's. And I must apologize to you here straight away -- I always try not to be too specific, for fear of being singled out.

This waiting room, it's not Doc's first, but it's similar to all the others he's had as he's moved around from building to building and office to office, around this whole small town, and I follow him. He's trying to run from something I presume. I hope he's not running from me. It doesn't seem to be me that he's running from. Not to me at least. Most people run from me. No one's hiding. Do I make sense? Perhaps I make sense to some. Perhaps I make more sense than anyone would care to admit. And it's not just Doc, people are always

　　　　J.L.Judd　　　Immediately Verifiable

trying to make a case of me. So…I try not to be too specific.
"Don't say anything," I always say. People are afraid of me.
Sometimes they're afraid of me, and I really don't know why.
It's all I see -- fear.

The walls are white, and the chairs are cheap and made
of bamboo whicker – out there in the waiting room. I've never
liked sitting out there, waiting, but I do it. There isn't much
for me to do. I listen to Beethoven. Mozart makes me sick –
and puke. Sitting in bamboo is hard enough, "Just like Doc."
Doc is just like everyone else. He hasn't figured IT out yet.
No one's figured IT out. Ahhh, the quintessential IT. I usually
bring a book to read while I wait, while I listen to Beethoven.
I'll turn Mozart off in my brain…for now…so I won't get sick.
I've gotten good at shutting myself off, turning it off, shutting
it all out. It used to take -- take two -- but not anymore. The
books I read are usually off the cheap rag classic rack, and
they're long enough, and Dostoyevsky could keep any person
busy for years upon years and that's who I'm reading for the
time being.

Doc's running late. He's usually running late. He's
running late today.

I have to fill out the form, "The magic form" as it's
called by Doc's assistant. It's just a blank piece of paper. His
assistant has been here as long as I've been here – she's never
changed either, just like the waiting room. "Fill out the magic
form," she says, and then I write down my drugs, and my
doses, and the times of day I take them. I've never figured it
out, what these medications are. I've been doing this for quite
a long time, for almost as long as Doc has been doing it, and
I've probably seen hundreds of patients come and go, and
definitely I've seen them fight, and flail, and scream, and run,
and hide…and bleed…sometimes. Most of the patients are

scared. "They're just scared," I tell myself, and I think it's a
fair diagnosis. I'm told most everybody's scared. I think
they're scared of me. But my drugs…my drugs help. I've
seen a hundred patients come and go, and as far as I can tell
while writing my doses and their most effective times of day,
that I must be dissociative. Doc always says I'm schizo-
something, but my medication says I'm dissociative. On the
magic form where Doc's assistant has written the word
"Diagnosis" it says 295.10. It's a DSM-IV code which stands
for schizophrenia, disorganized type. And then people call me
paranoid. I know better though, my meds tell me different, and
I think Doc must write 295.10 just for insurance reasons. I
think I'll cross it out, the 295.10, yes, and I'll write, this will be
funny, 300.6. The DSM-IV code 300.6 stands for
depersonalization disorder. It means I won't hurt anyone.
That I tend to think outside of myself. I'm quite disheveled
and, yes, disorganized. Doc will get a kick out of it.
Diagnoses, I've learned are made by any doctor just at that
time he or she sees a patient. A diagnosis is just a tool in
guiding treatment. The prognosis for 295.10, however, is not
so good. It would mean that they think my social skills are
degenerative. They must think that I'll get evermore socially
unacceptable. The diagnosis 300.6? I take my drugs, just like
I wrote them on the magic form – no different, not at all, and I
should be okay, aside from my pervasive "outside of the box"
thinking. But for Doc's sake, and for whatever reasons he has
(they must be good reasons I decided long ago) in dealing with
the insurance companies to make his assistant…oh, I'd call her
by name but I'm trying to avoid details…write
295.10…295.10…295.10…for his sake, I I try to pretend to be
schizo-something, or the other, just to make everyone happy. I
try to be social. I try to ease everyone's educated ego – not

                              J.L.Judd   Immediately Verifiable

just Doc's. I've been taught that I'm not that smart. I wrote "geodon" by where the word "Medications" had been written – I think "One God" when I see the word geodon. I write the low dose of trileptal I take – I've been told that the dose is not therapeutic -- it's such a small dose. But I take it, I take my drugs. I write adderall, and nuvigil – a dissociative – for dissociation – a deficit in attention -- to an extreme. Yes, my drugs they say one thing, they say to me that I'm dissociative, and not schizo-something or another.

Since that first day in court, I don't remember – "How did I get here?" The guy on the stand, it wasn't Doc, he called me schizo-something. The label just stuck. I'm a socially constructed self. I think he said bipolar with schizoid tendencies. Deluted. How am I supposed to remember what they called me when they call me deluted. I'm not supposed to remember, so don't ask, if I'm right when you ask what I am, it means I'm wrong. I'm deluted, so I don't know. Don't ask. Delusion. The courts are delusive. They ask me what the guy on the stand called me and if I know what it means. The question is what they call a Catch-22. How am I supposed to know.

Doc would probably say I'm "borderline" again if I asked him what I am, he wasn't the guy on the stand that first day in court. Borderline? It's ambiguous psychology. I can read. Ambiguous psychology must be like pseudo-psychosis. I've read the diagnoses. The Mayo Clinic is quite clear as to how schizoaffective is defined, and schizophrenia too, and dissociative, depersonalization, bipolar…the list goes on. They all have real clear definitions. I'll stick to 300.6 -- "Thinks that everyone else must be crazy for thinking that he or she might hurt someone." Doc will stick to 295.10. There's no such thing as "borderline" anything in real psychology as

    J.L.Judd   Immediately Verifiable

far as I can tell…but I appease his ego. I can read. I might be crazy. You can call me that. I'm not dumb.

A police siren just drove by outside, I can hear it. I'll get up. There's a firetruck behind out there. White painted wall across the alley. I look out the window to my left. There must have been an emergency.

"Are you done filling out the magic form?" The assistant came in a hurry when she saw me get up to look out the window.

"Yes. I think it's all right." I never know what to say to anyone. Sometimes what's going on in my head and what I say out loud are two entirely different things.

"He should be just another few minutes," the assistant is pleasant. I know better though. She's seen more patients than I've seen over the years. And she seems to have seen evil that I could never even dream. She's seen us all flail, fail, and cry, run. And I'm sure she's seen worse than me. All I'm wondering is "How am I 'borderline'?" I actually like to make the little quotes with my fingers when I think it, "Borderline!" No one knows what I'm thinking. What is that? I wonder. Part schizo, part bipolar, part dissociative. I must be dissociative, if there is such a thing. I think, no, it must be…I must be dissociative.

Who are these people? They're all crazy. What are these drugs they've got me on? Do they make me schizo. The people. Yes. It's the drugs. It's them. I'm not schizo. All my life, I've ever only heard terrible things about people with schizophrenia, but I never hurt anyone, and all I ever do is read. Classic rags, Dostoyevsky. What are we supposed to do, us "borderline" patients? They give us drugs. They call us names. We never hurt anyone. At least I never did hurt anyone. I wonder if Doc's a specialist treating people like me

              J.L.Judd   Immediately Verifiable

this way. I wonder why he calls me "Borderline." I love making the little quotes with my fingers when no one knows what I'm thinking. Either way, I know, I can't argue about being schizo-something or another with him. He knows those words better than I do. It's how they train their well-trained egos in the psychology classes. He's a doctor though and only took those psychology classes after the fact. He gives me drugs. I'm "Borderline". "I'm in recovery," I think to myself, and I have to make the quotes again for some reason, and I wonder for what reason.   I'm in recovery from a classic dissociation. I just throw my hands down to my sides and I shake my head.

"Get on with it. I'm not going through that again. You know I'm not making you psychotic. I'm not God." Doc's elation antagonized me – he's not God. "So tell me. What do you mean by a classic dissociation?"

"In the beginning I was at Wendy's. It was a long time ago. Dave Thomas was still hocking his Spicy Chicken Sandwich with little red horns like a devil drawn on each ad. I saw the ad pinned high overhead when I was in line. I ordered a Spicy Chicken Saandwich, maybe it was just to appease Mr. Thomas and his devil horns. And I sat down to eat. It was lunch outside the hospital on campus and the restaurant was full so I sat next to a stranger. We began to talk. The ads of Dave Thomas and his devil horns were still in clear view. The man I spoke with was a record producer. I told him that I'd just started playing the guitar, and that I played blues, and he told me to stay out of the record business. I looked at the ad, and I laughed, and I bit into my Spicy Chicken Sandwich, and I couldn't help but to think I must be sitting next to the devil

                         J.L.Judd   Immediately Verifiable

himself, incarnate. That's a classic dissociation. That's how my nervous breakdown started. I immediately began talking to God in my head. I knew what was really going on the whole time…that God doesn't talk…and that I wasn't sitting next to the devil incarnate. That's a classic dissociation, isn't it?"

"Hey Doc. How you been? You ready to see me now? How are things going? I haven't seen you in a while." I better just get in the office and sit down and shut up. At least the chairs are more comfortable in there – a leather sofa, big and fluffy, like clouds.

There's nothing too unusual. Everything is as I remember it. There are large plants, with spots showing up from the bases – down in their pots – there were spot lights. Everything is too ordinary, and I'm getting so used to things the way they are. I'll sit on the right side of the couch, facing Doc. I normally sit on the left. Doc has a grin on his face. My book can go right here on my left. His hair is a mess, his sport coat is worn thin, and his jeans are tattered at the cuff. Nothing's new. Though he's lost some weight. I've seen him heavy, and I've seen him thin. He looks happy, he looks sad. He's not like a glutton though. Tempestuous. The window over my shoulder, behind the place where I normally sit, that window in his office is open. I wonder why it's open. I look around the room and I wonder why it's open. What must I have done to end up here? I must have done something wrong. Something's terribly wrong. 300.6. No one believes me. "I never went to medical school," I quickly think.

"I see you sat on the left side of the couch today." Doc was serious. It was sudden, he was no longer rosy and alive.

"Uhhh. Yeah. But let's not talk about that. How are you feeling today? What have you been up to lately? Have

    J.L.Judd   Immediately Verifiable

you done anything interesting? I see you've lost some weight.
Is there something on your mind? You looked quite happy
when I first sat down. You looked extraordinarily happy.
Your cheeks were pink, and I could see your teeth. Your hair
looks as though you've forgotten all the troubles of the world.
And I believe you. I know you've known nothing but troubles
in this place. Tell me. What's going on?" I think it would be
best if I try to attend to it. Attend to whatever it is. Maybe if I
straighten my arms at my knees. No. My hands, put them
between my knees. No, not like that either. At my sides? My
hands at my sides. How do I sit? What's this situation I'm in?
I can't even look at him, he's lost so much weight. I look at
my hands. "What was that? I didn't hear you? Did you
say…did you say there's somewhere else you need to be?"

"I can't see you as a patient anymore."

     J.L.Judd   Immediately Verifiable

Annotated Bibliography

Burgess, A. (1986). *A Clockwork Orange*. New York, London: W.W. Norton Company.

Burgess Is critical of psychology in this work, more specifically of operant conditioning and behavior modification that might be associated with conforming to society. The book is banned on shelves throughout the world. He uses examples of both abnormal and criminal behavior, and he arbitrarily but uniformly replaces certain words (nouns and adjectives) referring to abnormal social behavior to give the reader an uneasy feeling about deviant society.

Calhoon, A. (2001). Factors Affecting the Reading of Rimes in Words and Nonwords in Beginning Readers with Cognitive Disabilities: Explorations in Similarity and Difference in Word Recognition Cue Use. Journal of Autism and Developmental Disorders. 31(5), 491-504. (Document ID: 200100442004).

Calhoon explores different aspects of rhyming words, as well as the ability of people with various disabilities, each having their own deviant linguistics patterns, to recognize rhyming words from lists. It will be used to develop a character diagnosed with schizophrenia that might use specific kinds of rhyming (medium frequency) in his or her speech.

Dostoevsky, F. (2003). *Notes From the Underground*. New York, NY: Barnes and Noble Classics. (Original Work published 1864).

Dostoevsky's books have been banned throughout the world, in various place, for about a century and a half. "Notes from the Underground" is a first person narrative with a socially deviant narrator. Examples of his use of run-on sentences to create uneasiness in the reader will be most helpful.

Fodor, J. (2006). How the mind works: what we still don't know. Daedalus, 135(3), 86-94. Retrieved February 6, 2011, from Research Library Core. (Document ID: 1110756781).

Fodor explores the cognitive side of linguistics. Cognition will be important because of my narrator's skewed perspective of reality and how that should reflect in the character's semantics. There should very little heuristic quality about the demeanor of such a character.

Gibson, T. (2011). Make it up—or Keep It Real?. The Writer, 124(3), 38-9. Retrieved from OmniFile Full Text Select database.

Gibson poses the obvious question of whether a writer of fiction should use a real or a "make-believe" setting, and describes the differences therein. The usefulness of such an article in writing fiction should be self-evident. I will be using a make-believe setting.

Kasper, G. Four perspectives on L2 pragmatic development Applied Linguistics (2001) 22(4): 502-530 doi:10.1093/applin/22.4.502.

Pragmatism is explored from various aspects, and defined here. It is a useful subject because a character with schizophrenia will be lacking most typical pragmatic ability. Likewise, a doctor might be pragmatic to a fault.

Haddon, M. (2004). *The Curious Incident of the Dog in the Night-Time*. New York, NY: Random House.

Haddon's book is an excellent example of what I might be attempting to mimic some aspects of. He wrote a first-person narrative from the perspective of a character with autism. His character is believable, and unsettling in his innocent appeal to the reader.

Mikhailov, D., Emel'yanov, G., & Stepanova, N. (2009). Formation and clustering of noun contexts within the framework of splintered values. Pattern Recognition and Image Analysis, 19(4), 664-672. Retrieved January 23, 2011, from ABI/INFORM Global. (Document ID: 1923038171).

This article dives deeper into cognition and linguistics – namely pattern recognition. A character with schizophrenia will have

    J.L.Judd   Immediately Verifiable

obvious trouble avoiding patterns that might seem unacceptable to most people in society, whether those patterns are syntactic or behavioral. Most people tend to recognize patterns easily and avoid all but the most complicated of them. A person with schizophrenia cannot easily avoid simple patterns.

Nabokov, V. (1955). *Lolita*. New York, NY: Random House.

Nabokov's "Lolita" is one of the most banned books in America. It has been banned in the entire state of Ohio. The main character is the quintessential deviant, a criminal, a murderer, a child-molester, a kidnapper, a rapist, etc. and he appears to hardly notice it. Nabokov's use of complicated semantics to cover up what would otherwise be sexual innuendo and profanity is exquisite. He uses no profane language throughout the book, and the reader is left aberrant. It will be helpful to develop the doctor's ego and language as the doctor will appear sinister to the narrator with the illness.

Nicolof, M. (2009). MENTAL STATES, LANGUAGE, AND COMPOSITIONALITY. Linguistic and Philosophical Investigations, 8, 176-181. Retrieved January 23, 2011, from ProQuest Religion. (Document ID: 2084354471).

This article further explores the linguistics associated with both primitive and complex concepts as well as cognition. It will be useful in expressing the differences between the cognitive abilities of the doctor and the narrator.

Scovel, T. (2010). *Psycholinguistics*. Oxford: Oxford University Press.

Scovel's book is an exploration into various aspects of psycholinguistics, the development and acquisition of language, language loss, and abnormal patterns found throughout linguistics studies. It will be profoundly helpful in writing my story. Scovel has included examples of dialogue of people with schizophrenia, as well as given many examples of improper syntax that people find entirely unacceptable.

　　J.L.Judd　　Immediately Verifiable

Steslow, K. (2010). Metaphors in Our Mouths: The Silencing of the
Psychiatric Patient. The Hastings Center Report, 40(4), 30-3.
Retrieved April 6, 2011, from Research Library Core. (Document
ID: 2096486691).

*The use of metaphors in assessing the self within the constructs of
society are explored as they are used in the field of psychology.
New patterns of thinking can emerge when logical patterns are
discovered within meaningful use of metaphors by patients who
normally are lacking in structured patterns of logical thought. The
application of such a theory in this short story should not have to
be explained.*

Strong, T., & Sutherland, O. (2007). Conversational Ethics in
Psychological Dialogues: Discursive and Collaborative
Considerations. Canadian Psychology, 48(2), 94-105. (Document
ID: 10.1037/cp2007011).

*Conversational Ethics in Psychological Dialogues explores the
patterns of dialogues and the ethics associated with those dialogues
between therapists and their patients. It will be useful in making
the doctor appear to be unethical to the reader from the narrator's
point of view, which will be useful in upsetting the established
order of things.*

Sun, H. (2010). The Cognitive Study of Metaphor and its
Application in English Language Teaching/L'ÉTUDE COGNITIVE
DE LA MÉTAPHORE ET SON APPLICATION DANS
L'ENSEIGNEMENT DE L'ANGLAIS. Canadian Social Science,
6(4), 175-9. Retrieved from OmniFile Full Text Select database.

*The two different types of metaphor are studied in this article. It
will be useful as a majority of our established society finds
linguistics metaphors to be genius sometimes, inappropriate at
other times, and even deviant if used in incorrect context. It might
be useful for both characters to be saying one thing while actually
talking about something else, and quite possibly it will add much
needed humor if it can be assumed that both characters are
referring to different things.*

On the Relation of Research and Theory

On the Relation of Theory and Research

It seems quite critical that most people working in an academic setting should have a well developed understanding of the relationship between the concepts of *research* and *theory*. Such an understanding should also prove useful to those same people should they continue into corporate and other working environments thereafter. Both theory and research are found to be necessary when analyzing hypothetical situations while determining the possible causes and effects of any occurrence within a given set of circumstances; and because the two concepts seem to be so intimately related it seems quite necessary to define both terms – *research* and *theory*, to distinguish each from the other during such a process, and also to investigate the components which seem to make the concepts of theory and research key factors in determining one another.

Technically, during the accepted method of discovery, research would follow any initial *hypothesis*; a hypothesis being little more than a "best guess" postulated from observed phenomenon, concept, or even simply from an idea of the way things ought to be, merely a prediction still lacking in corresponding evidence when considering sets of observed circumstances. This subsequent research, which is the process of analyzing and gathering data to ultimately determine a theory, or a broad and general explanation of the phenomenon first questioned in order to predict a phenomenon, exercise control of it, or to ultimately stimulate some kind of social change, would then follow the hypothesis. The next of goal of

                J.L.Judd   Immediately Verifiable

researchers, in most respects, is to try and further prove, or disprove, their initial theory by testing the validity of that theory, once it's found, with further research that might, or might not, lead to another lying in opposition or as a corollary to the first. To clarify, a theory is based on research, after which that same theory perpetuates the research process, and the further research can potentially generate alternate theories; the only requisites seem to be that the nature of all research is analytical and that all analysis can be considered research. That analysis is always empirical and conducted by relating data gathered from observed phenomenon, from experiment, or from history should be fundamental. Depending on the quality of the research then, in constructing theory, analysis can often be conducted through research writing and not only through empirical analysis using formula; however, in either case the process of relating, grouping, and classifying with the intention of further investigating constituent parts of any observed or learned phenomenon (Kant, 1855), a process which can always be repeated with any need for further inquiry, seems to be required regardless of whether such analysis is quantitative or qualitative.

According to Dewey, "…theory is nothing but a scheme or plan of action, and therefore truth is nothing but the successfulness of the idea" (Deen, P., 2001). It can be deduced then that the end of any theory must have social value to some degree, and it should be noted that individual perspective, because it is rooted in social construct with respect to social value, always proves to be quite important. Marcuse stresses that an individual's perspective within a society even necessitates theory by saying that, "Individual rationality has developed into efficient compliance with the pre-given continuum of means and ends" (Deen, P., 2011), in other

     J.L.Judd   Immediately Verifiable

words a theory cannot exist without some perspective having been determined by social values. Theories are general explanations that concern phenomenon which have been removed from the certain objectives used in research, and it can be said, so removed from objectivity, that theories have "no immediate practical application" (Deen, P., 2011). It is also supported that such criterion hold true for all theories, no matter if the research conducted is quantitative, as it likely would be concerning research in the physical sciences, or qualitative, as would be necessary for research conducted in social sciences.

Again however, qualitative analysis is found to be important to research in all sciences – physical science, social science, as well as humanities; although those qualitative effects that could result in ambiguity are tending to be much diminished in their consideration by the purest physical sciences while those same qualitative concerns, which were shown here prior to be important because of social construct and perspective, are becoming increasingly determinant of research conducted in the social sciences, and even more so in the humanities. Quite often qualitative research is conducted with the practice of what is called "Library research," and it need not directly concern subjects in a study. This "Library research" is based on sources of phenomenon that aren't observed first hand and so they are called secondary, not primary, sources in research. Secondary sources are used in analyzing not only opposing theories that might have been concluded by other researchers, but they are readily used in analyzing history when researching social behavior of groups, as well in case studies in medical research and psychology.

Ultimately we find that theory and research are closely entwined, though not inseparable. Research seems

                    J.L.Judd   Immediately Verifiable

fundamentally based in action – that action being that of
analysis, and then we find theory to be the abstraction of the
result of such analysis, as it is removed from the objects of
research and theory, and it remains as a framework of
expectations in the observable world and is provided for
individuals under some corresponding sets of circumstances.
In the end we see that theories are based on research that has
been initiated by some observed phenomenon quite dependent
on perspective, while they stimulate further research leading to,
in many instances, opposing or correlating theories, to more
expectations, thus to further research.

  J.L.Judd   Immediately Verifiable

References

Deen, P. (2011). Dialectical vs. Experimental Method: Marcuse's Review of Dewey's Logic: The Theory of Inquiry. *Charles S. Peirce Society. Transactions of the Charles S. Peirce Society*. Retrieved October 12, 2010 from http://www.proquest.com.

Kant, I. (1855). *Critique of Pure Reason*. (J. Meiklejohn, Trans.). London: Henry G. Bohn, York Street, Covent Garden.

Keegan, S. (2009). Practitioner Perspectives 'Emergent Inquiry'. *Qualitative Market Research: An International Journal*. Retrieved October 6, 2010 from http://www.emeraldinsight.com/1352-2752.htm.

Russell, C., Wink, D., & Weaver, G. (2008). Inquiry-based and Research-based Laboratory Pedagogies in Undergraduate Science. *Nature Chemical Biology*. Retrieved October 6, 2010 from http://www.nature.com/naturechemicalbiology.

Philosophy of Leadership

Leadership is the quality necessarily found in a leader. It is a skill that can be nurtured from childhood, if not simply learned in adulthood. It centers a person, a leader, within others and within circumstances. He or she will emerge from within a group as both circumstances and group form, and quite often, against the accepted norms and mores of some society at large. The leader will gradually emerge from within such a group, will be placed in that position, and will draw his or her authority from a group of followers because of virtue, integrity, learned ability, and ethical choice, i.e. whatever humane qualities have been found requisite for the situation. Despite adversity, and often against great odds, a leader will create change. He or she will have some vision, an ideal, some abstraction that the people from whom he or she has emerged will strive to attain. With that in mind, because we have all evolved as social beings, history has shown that the greatest leaders are champions of the ideal qualities of humanity which have been found to possibly exist within any society; those ideals we've labeled with terms such as freedom, and liberty, and equality, and even Peace. A group of followers must believe that their leader can bring them to such ends in order to have effective leadership in place.

      Leadership requires attention to diversity. Opinions, often foreign to a leader, must be considered in leadership as others follow him or her in attaining something better than their selves, to attaining whatever that group's goal decidedly has been that has placed any leader in his or her role. A leader will be benevolent, always remembering that he or she is merely one of the group from which he or she has emerged.

       J.L.Judd   Immediately Verifiable

Despite what's been said, blind people will tend to follow some person who has once been blind. Leadership requires the ability to remain focused on that shared goal of a group, while delegating work that has to be done, in order to attain that goal, to his or her followers. Leadership requires the ability to be reasonable and rational, while knowing what can be expected of others, and not forcibly changing those others as people. Leadership is a process, and it must never be forgotten that leadership, and its quality, is necessarily decided by some group of people who willingly become followers, and that it seems to be human nature that people cannot generally be coerced, or forced, into choosing their leadership without some recourse or revolt. And as we are all human, it seems our nature to commonly know that effective leadership can only be that which will bring any group to its understood and agreed upon goal. That goal is what gives a group its value, its purpose, and its meaning.

Leadership is a rite bestowed on a person by others, for the benefit of those others, as they try against all odds to overcome adversity and become better in the future than what they are in the present as a whole. Leadership is a power granted by the people. Leadership is guidance through much needed and, sometimes, inevitable change. Leadership is the necessary result of circumstance and situation, both which are often sadly the spawn of tragedy. Leadership is humility in the face of egoism, as well as egoism in the face of humility. Leadership is the cornerstone of people existing together as social beings. Leadership has become, it always has been, and it always will be, as elusive as it is necessary.

J.L.Judd   Immediately Verifiable